W9-CNC-674

LEADER'S GUIDE

SEEING WITH THE HEART

How to Be Spiritual in an Unspiritual World

Rev. Dr. Johnnie William Skinner, Sr.

Urban Ministries, Inc.
chicago, illinois

Publisher
Urban Ministries, Inc.
Chicago, Illinois
(312) 233-4499

First Edition
First Printing
ISBN: 0-940955-33-4
Catalog No. 9-6301

....

DEDICATION

This book is dedicated to the memory of
my brother Tom Skinner, whose life and ministry
inspired my vision and mission for the Church
and the African American community.

Johnnie William Skinner, Sr.

ACKNOWLEDGMENTS

I would like to acknowledge the following persons for their guidance and help in my spiritual journey. I thank my parents, the late Reverend Alester J. Skinner and Georgia Skinner, whose faith in the Lord and compassion for people made the difference in the direction of my life.

I would like to thank Reverend Stanley B. Long of the South Bay Community Church in California; Dr. William E. Pannell of Fuller Theological Seminary, Pasadena, California; and Reverend Dr. Samuel DeWitt Proctor, who served as my mentor at the United Theological Seminary in Dayton, Ohio. A special word of thanks to my pastor the Reverend Dr. Gardner Calvin Taylor for helping me to understand the importance of prayer in my life and ministry, and to the late Reverend Dr. M.L. Wilson of the Convent Avenue Baptist Church, New York City for the opportunity to serve in that church while a student at Union Theological Seminary in New York City.

Thank you, also to my friends in the ministry of Jesus Christ: the Reverends Calvin O. Butts, III, Charles S. Brown, Frederick C. Ennette, Daryl Ward, Ron Ballard, Joseph R. Hickman, Jr., Edward L. Wheeler, Margaret Mallory, Prathia Hall Wynn, Kevin M. Turman, Charles E. Booth, Charles A. McKinney, Lee Johnson and Mr. Christopher H. Woodhull.

My thanks and appreciation to my administrative assistant, Deborah S. Barnes for allowing the Lord to use her gifts for the English language in making possible the original work which served as the basis for this work. A word of thanks to Denise Gates, who served as the editor for this book.

••

I must thank the people of the Mount Zion Baptist Church of Knoxville, Tennessee for their prayerful support of this ministry.

A special word of thanks and appreciation to my spouse, Andrea, and my three sons: Johnnie, Calvin Taylor, and Thomas Corey for their love, support and patience.

I pray that this book will find meaning in the lives of those who read it. May the Lord of the Church receive all of the honor, glory, and praise.

TABLE OF CONTENTS

FOREWORD

Too long, too often, performance and prayer have been separated, attitude and action divorced. So! we have held the notion that if one is contemplative and prayerful, one cannot be assertive and active in the struggle for a better life.

This fine treatise seeks with resounding success to wipe out this dichotomy. If we had read the Gospel discerningly, we would have avoided this sad, and often fatal, separation. If we read the Gospel carefully we will discover that proper prayer produces performances, mandates it.

As we approach the climactic moments of our Lord's life, there is a brief but endlessly moving and instructive word about the joining of quiet, mystic communion to the noise and strife of life's great disputed passages, its momentous confrontations. At the end of the last supper, Matthew says they sang a hymn—contemplation, and went out into the great cosmic struggle with evil—crucifixion. Johnnie Skinner, appropriately enough, summons us in this book to see and accept this union of worship and work, prayer and performance, contemplation and confrontation.

Dr. Gardner C. Taylor, Senior Pastor Emeritus
The Concord Baptist Church of Christ
Brooklyn, New York

9

PREFACE

Seeing With the Heart examines the expression of spirituality in the African American Church as demonstrated through preaching, worship, and discipline. Within this context, the book discusses how spirituality is meant for both the interior and exterior life of today's African American Church. It is hoped that this study will lead to an ongoing exploration of the all-but-untapped potential and power of spiritual reality within the African American Christian Church.

Objectives. Upon completion of this book, the reader should be able to discuss how spirituality relates to the identity of both the believer and the Church. Questions such as who we are, why we exist, and what we want to do can be best answered with the understanding that God is in every area of our lives. Knowing our spiritual self-identity is essential to the fulfillment of the mission of the Church in this time. A goal of this book is to encourage the examination and discovery of who we are spiritually so that we can become more effective in what we do as people of God.

Organization. This book is divided into 12 chapters. Each chapter is based on a sermon given by the author, the Reverend Dr. Johnnie William Skinner, Sr., to his congregation at Mount Zion Baptist Church in Knoxville, Tennessee. The chapters are divided into three sections: an introduction, the sermon, and three, different sets of Bible study questions. The Bible Study Application section allows the participants to examine what the Word of God has to say about the topic of each chapter. The Personal Ministry section encourages the participants to look at their personal lives in light of the Word of God. Finally, the Church Ministry section prompts participants to develop new ideas to improve the ministry of the Church.

Uses. This book can be used in a variety of ways. It can be used for private or group study. It can also be used in the local church for training of teachers and deacons, Sunday School electives, Training Hour curriculum, weekday Bible studies, adult Vacation Bible School curriculum as well as in family devotions. The following paragraphs describe just a few of many possible techniques which can be used to make your study of *Seeing With the Heart* come alive.

Group Study—90-Minute Sessions. This book is designed for a two-part group study session. The participants should be encouraged to read each chapter in preparation for the sessions. In Part One of the session, participants examine the Scripture and discuss the introduction and the sermon that follows. This discussion would require about 35 minutes. Then, in Part Two, the session leader divides the group into smaller groups to answer and discuss the Bible Study Application questions.

The small group discussions provide each participant with an opportunity to contribute to the group's understanding and application of the material. About 25 minutes should be allowed for small groups to answer the questions. In the final group discussion, for about 30 minutes, the participants reconvene with the larger group and report their findings.

Group Study—60-Minute Sessions. In shorter periods, it might be necessary to use part of the chapter as a stimulus for discussion during the group meeting itself. The other part of the chapter might be used as a "homework" assignment or for private devotional study.

Church-Wide Retreats and Leadership Training. If all or part of a weekend is available for studying the book, it can be explored in a number of ways. For example, 12 leaders could each be assigned a different chapter. Participants would be encouraged to read the entire book prior to the retreat or scheduled training. They might also be encouraged to select a chapter to study in depth and then enroll in the session devoted to that chapter.

In the opening session, the overall leader (pastor, minister, special speaker, or lay leader) would give a presentation based on Chapter One to set the tone and focus of the study. This presentation could be general (exploring historical and contemporary issues of African American spirituality), or specific (challenging participants to examine and apply the information to the local church body).

After the opening session, participants would attend small group sessions that focus on a particular chapter for the entire weekend. These sessions should include general discussion, personal application, and produce specific suggestions or strategies for church ministry.

The final session would be devoted to small group discussion and reports. These reports should be given by representatives from each small group. This final discussion would involve sharing the answers to the Church Ministry Application section of each chapter. These suggestions may be used to plan activities for the upcoming church year.

Family Devotions. During the week preceding the study of a given chapter, each member would read the chapter privately and select a different question from the exercise for study. In devotions, the family would first discuss the introduction and sermon. Then each member would read the assigned question and present his or her opinion "round robin style." The family discussion could follow each question or be reserved until the end. The devotion should end with personal application and prayer.

The Leader's Guide. This leader's guide is designed to assist you in facilitating large and small group discussion of the book *Seeing With the Heart*. The leader's guide contains a preface and 12 lesson plans—one for each chapter in the student book. Each lesson plan includes objectives, suggested topics for prayer, questions to help the participants examine the Scripture, guidelines for chapter discussions, and instructions for large and small group discussions. The leader's guide also contains answers to the Bible Study Application questions.

Leading the Discussion. There are several techniques which can be effectively used to lead discussions in a church setting. A discussion leader can:

- Study the material to be presented beforehand.
- Look up the verses as you read through the material.
- Present background information on the topic before the discussion.
- Take steps to relax the participants.
- Avoid embarrassing people.
- Keep the discussion moving.
- Reword statements that the participants may not understand.
- Prevent anyone from monopolizing the discussion or straying from the topic.
- Encourage the expression of feelings and "down to earth" discussion (discourage intellectualizing).
- Use humor to reduce tension.
- Ask good questions.

• Keep in mind that the most effective discussion leader of all time is our Lord Jesus Christ. By studying His manner of dealing with the woman at the well, Nicodemus, Peter, and others, much can be learned.

Preparing Participants for the Discussion. Chapter One, "Spiritual Exploration" provides a foundation for the chapters which follow. Be sure that all participants read this chapter. After the first meeting for the class, encourage the students to read the material for each session beforehand. Different participants can be assigned to answer different questions from the Bible Study Application and the Church Ministry Application sections at the end of each chapter. In this way, the participants can be well-informed when they approach the discussion. The additional time to prepare may also improve the depth and detail of the ideas exchanged.

Aim of This Study *(Introduction to the Sermons)*

The aim of this study is to develop a framework in which the people of God can begin to define and explore their spirituality. The book took its shape by way of 12 sermons delivered over a period of time to the congregation of Mount Zion Baptist Church of Knoxville, Tennessee. These sermons, in many ways, represent a spiritual journey. More than words, they were also experiences colored by the context in which they were preached—the African American worship experience. The sermons, in and of themselves, could never be a cure-all for the spiritual ills of a congregation. They have, nevertheless, served as a beginning toward spiritual wholeness and health.

In the same manner, it is hoped that this study will help other African American congregations recognize that there is a need for spiritual renewal and growth, and provide new insights into the life of the Church and how the Holy Spirit empowers us to become more like Christ and less like the world. As we come to know who we are, we will be able to move toward a new understanding of our mission and ministry.

....

CHAPTER ONE

SPIRITUAL EXPLORATION

Lesson format for sessions of 90 minutes or more:

PART ONE		PART TWO	
ACTIVITY	TIME	ACTIVITY	TIME
Opening Prayer	5 min.	Small Group Study	20 min.
Scripture Reading	5 min.	Large Group Presentations	20 min.
Scripture Search	5 min.	Large Group Discussion	10 min.
Chapter Highlights	20 min.	Closing Prayer	5 min.

For sessions of less than 90 minutes, use PART ONE only and assign the Bible Study Application section as homework.

LESSON AIMS: At the end of this two-part session, the participant should be able to: a) define the terms "church," "spirituality," "worship," and "discipline" from both a biblical and historical perspective; b) understand who we are spiritually; c) discuss the mission of the African American Church in the world today.

I. PART ONE

A. OPENING PRAYER

Open the session with prayer. Include the request that each participant would receive the following:

- A greater understanding of our unique spiritual identity.
- An awareness of the role and importance of worship.
- Increased insight into the significance of our role and mission in the world today.

B. SCRIPTURE SEARCH

1. Ask someone to read John 4:23-24 aloud to the group.
2. Ask for volunteers to answer the following questions:
   a) Who do you think Jesus means when He speaks of true worshipers worshiping "in spirit"?
      Answers will vary.
   b) What spirit do you think He was speaking of?
      The Holy Spirit.
   c) Why do you think the Holy Spirit is important?
      Answers will vary.

C. CHAPTER HIGHLIGHTS

To be effective, the African American Church must understand its mission in the present-day world and in the local community. However, before a congregation can understand the mission of the Church, it must come to know and understand its spiritual self-identity. This chapter provides the contextual and theological foundation for the chapters which follow.

Using Chapter One as background, give a general overview of the chapter. You may want to use the chapter's introduction as a starting point. Be sure to include the following topics:

1. Why Context Is Important
2. History of African American Worship
3. Elements of Worship
4. Spiritual Discipline
5. Spiritual Direction

II. PART TWO
A. BIBLE STUDY APPLICATION

1. Introduction

   The Bible Study Application section contains 14 questions that provide a contextual and theological foundation for the chapters which follow. The discussion of the Bible Study Application questions should confirm that the students understand the basic definitions and concepts and foster a climate in which people feel comfortable sharing their opinion.

   Allow as much time as necessary to encourage free participation and exchange of opinions. Use the information preceding each set of questions to help introduce or close the discussion of a topic. Refer to the Bible references to help keep the discussion on track. Depending on the size and personality of the group, you can discuss as many or as few of the questions as needed.

2. Procedure

Select Small Group Leaders. Ask for volunteers or select five small group leaders. Then assign each small group leader a number from 1-5. (This can also be done beforehand to save time.) Ask the small group leaders to write their numbers on large sheets of white paper so that they can be seen from a distance.

Divide into Small Groups. Inform the participants that they will be separated into five small groups. Each group will study a different set of questions and then will present their findings to the larger group at the end of the study period. The questions should be assigned as follows:

Group #1: Defining the Church (questions 1-3)

Group #2: Elements of Worship (questions 4-6)

Group #3: Defining Spirituality (questions 7-8)

Group #4: Understanding the Past and Present (questions 9-11)

Group #5: Facing the Future (questions 12-14)

Allow Participants to Count Off by Fives. Then ask them to follow the small group leader who is holding their assigned number. Identify the location of each group. (These locations can also be pre-printed on a sheet of paper, photocopied, and distributed to save time.) Participants should then assemble into smaller groups in their respective meeting areas.

B. SMALL GROUP STUDY

1. Small Group Leaders

Each group will have one topic to explore. For each topic, there are several questions and related Scripture references to stimulate discussion.

2. Sharing Insights

After 15 minutes, designate someone who will summarize the small group discussion within the larger body of participants. Remind the designated person that she or he will only have five minutes to present.

C. LARGE GROUP PRESENTATIONS

Reconvene the Group. Call the small groups back together.

Explain the Procedure. Explain that a representative of each small group will share that group's reflections on the Bible Study Application questions with the larger group.

Remind Small Group Representatives of the Time. Remind each group representative that he or she should try to summarize the group's discussion in five minutes. Allow up to five minutes to discuss each group's presentation.

D. LARGE GROUP STUDY*

Church Ministry Discussion. The Church Ministry section contains three questions which address the implications for the local church. If time permits, the larger group can then discuss the Church Ministry questions together.

1. Introduction

   Give each participant a copy of the church's mission statement or statement of faith (or it can be read aloud to the group). This statement will be the basis of the Church Ministry discussion.

2. Sharing Insights

   This discussion should be open-ended and voluntary. The sharing of personal insights or recommendations for church ministry should be encouraged but not required. The group may have quite a bit to say. Watch the clock! Stop them after 10 minutes.

*Answers are not provided for the Church Ministry section because of the personal or specific nature of the questions.

E. PREPARATION FOR NEXT MEETING

Assignment. Have the participants read Chapter Two, "The Trials of Life" and review the questions in preparation for next week's session. Encourage them to come to the next session prepared to share their insights on the content of the chapter.

You may also want to assign small groups or questions to facilitate next week's meeting time.

F. CLOSING PRAYER

Hold hands, form a circle, and ask for specific prayer requests. Then ask for several volunteers to pray, keeping the prayer requests in mind.

ANSWERS TO BIBLE STUDY APPLICATION

Who Are We?

(Defining Church, Spirituality, Worship, and Discipline)
When we think of the Church, of what do we think? Do we think of an institution, a social organization, a social club, a political organization, or an economic order? What images of the Church are conjured in our minds? Thoughts of revival services, Sunday School, BTU, BYF, or various other activities that over the years have meant church. For many, church is one of the activities on a list of "things to do today." Often, people outside the church could care less about what we do inside. In many circles, the church is seen as being irrelevant and archaic. How should we define the Church? Let's begin by looking to see what the Word of God has to say.

Using the Scripture verses as a foundation for your answers, describe how the Bible defines or explains the following terms.

1. What is the Church?
   The Bible speaks of the Church in terms of people who are committed to Jesus Christ. The New Testament word used for the Church is *ecclesia* which means "called out." The Church is the body of Christ. Christ is the Head of the Church; Christ is in charge of the Church. Christ died for the Church, and we belong to Him.

2. Why does the Church exist?
   Contrary to popular misconceptions, we do not exist

for ourselves; we are to bring glory and honor to Jesus Christ, who is the Head of the Church.

3. Why is the worship experience important?

The spirituality of African American people emanates from their understanding of the worship experience. Without a doubt, worship in the African American Church leads to an understanding of the "who-ness" of God, the incarnation and resurrection of Jesus Christ, and the power and presence of the Holy Spirit in the midst of the people.

4. Describe the role of music in the African American worship experience.

The worship music of African Americans affirms the value of the worshiper. It creates an atmosphere that uplifts and inspires the worshipers to find release and relief from the everyday pressures and stresses of life. It also helps promote a better understanding of the work and will of God.

5. Describe the role of prayer in the African American worship experience.

Prayer is a privilege granted by God because of the work of redemption through Jesus Christ. Prayer is communicating the deepest needs and desires of the heart before an all-powerful, loving, and merciful God who hears and answers prayer. It invites the power of God to work in the life of the believer.

6. Describe the role of the sermon in the African American worship experience.

The preaching of the sermon is the empowering event of the worship service. The Word of God provides the power, force, and authority needed to motivate and enable the worshiper. Through the Spirit of God, the Word brings healing, conviction, and deliverance. It is also calls the people to faith, repentance, and greater service in the name of the risen Lord.

7. What is spirituality?

Spirituality is defined as the abiding presence of the Holy Spirit in both the inner life of the believer and in the atmosphere of the worship experience.

8. What is spiritual discipline?

Spiritual discipline involves the "working out" of our faith in everyday practice. It also affects how we respond to the social and political issues of our day. Through the power of the Holy Spirit, the people of God can become the catalyst for change in society.

Where Do We Come From?
(Is History Really Important?)
From its inception, the African American Christian Church has been on a journey of faith. From the very beginning, the African American believer possessed an indomitable spirit which held on to the vision of a better tomorrow until the reality of a new day of freedom dawned. Even in the midst of civil strife and unrest in this country, the African American Church continued to seek out and act on its mission as the people of God.

9. Why is the expression of spirituality within the African American Christian Church distinctive?

25

The spirituality of African American people is distinctive because of the uniqueness of the suffering and oppression borne by African Americans in this country.

10. Describe how earlier traditions affect the music, prayer, and preaching of today's worship experience.

To fully grasp who we are, we must recognize the traditions of the African American worship experience and how those traditions have been translated into today's worship. Because of our African heritage, African American worship involves the rhythm of dance and music. These African traditions as well as the experience and conditions of slavery became the basis for the "Negro spiritual." Today, some of these same patterns have been adapted and changed to meet current musical needs. In many congregations, the Wednesday evening prayer meeting provides the same warm, intimate setting which was characteristic of an earlier time. Similarly, the role of the African American preacher as community leader remains; his or her sermons must speak to the needs of the people by providing information as well as inspiration.

11. Discuss the legacy of leadership that brought the African American Church to this place and time.

We know that the African American Church has a good foundation upon which to build. Our sense of God in Jesus Christ was not developed in a vacuum, but with the prayers, hopes, aspirations, and desires of people who had nothing, but who possessed everything. Discussion should focus on the practical qualities (the importance of vision, commitment, courage) and the tangible results of leadership of men and women like Jesus Christ, Rev. Dr. Martin Luther King Jr., Rev. Addie Wyatt, Rev. Jesse Jackson, Mary McLeod Bethune, etc.

What Are We to Do?

(Whose Job Is It? Defining Roles and Responsibilities)
To our dismay, the African American Church of today is becoming increasingly distant from the mainstream of the African American community. In today's economy, many churches have been forced to turn their focus toward making mortgage payments. Oftentimes, due to the need to make these payments, the church becomes unable to develop significant ministries that would take its members beyond its doors. God's people must begin to sense and act on the belief that now is the time to move away from a mortgage mentality to ministry development, both internally and externally.

The Church must become spiritually prepared to do what God has called us to do in the future. The pastors and people of generations past have brought us to this moment and we cannot allow it to pass us by. The need is great, and we have the Source and resources available to us to do God's will.

12. Identify the challenges of meeting the physical needs of a diverse population. Discuss the similarity of human spiritual needs.
    Today's African American community is as diverse as any to be found elsewhere in this country. There

are highly trained professionals, educators, administrators, engineers, managers, and those who work in numerous other aspects of community life, as well as general laborers, service workers, the unemployed, and the homeless. However, although physical needs may vary, basic human spiritual needs are the same.

13. What is the role of the African American Church?

According to the Word and the will of God, we must become the salt, light, ambassadors, workers, witnesses, servants, conquerors, and overcomers in this world.

14. Discuss the importance of the vision or mission of the church.

The continued spiritual development of the African American Church will depend on the willingness and ability to develop new strategies and explore new spiritual possibilities. However, before we can develop a strategy or take effective action, we must know what we are trying to accomplish. Whenever the Church loses sight of its vision and purpose as a people of God, the spirit of the Church is weakened.

CHAPTER TWO

THE TRIALS OF LIFE

Lesson format for sessions of 90 minutes or more:

PART ONE		PART TWO	
ACTIVITY	TIME	ACTIVITY	TIME
Opening Prayer	5 min.	Small Group Study	20 min.
Scripture Reading	5 min.	Large Group Presentations	20 min.
Scripture Search	5 min.	Large Group Discussion	10 min.
Chapter Highlights	20 min.	Closing Prayer	5 min.

For sessions of less than 90 minutes, use PART ONE only and assign the Bible Study Application section as homework.

LESSON AIMS: At the end of this two-part session, the participant should be able to: a) provide an overview of the biblical account of Jesus' temptation in the wilderness; b) discuss the types of temptation which we face today; c) identify the spiritual weapons and resources that we can use to overcome temptation.

I. PART ONE
A. OPENING PRAYER

Open the session with prayer. Include the request that each participant would receive the following:

- An understanding of Jesus' temptation in the wilderness as related in the Scripture.
- The knowledge needed to apply these biblical principles and examples today.
- The development of insight, wisdom, and practical strategies for overcoming temptation in the future.

B. SCRIPTURE SEARCH

1. Ask someone to read Matthew 4:1-11 aloud to the group.
2. Ask for volunteers to answer the following questions:
   a) Who led Jesus into the wilderness to be tempted?
      The Holy Spirit
   b) Who was tempting Jesus?
      The devil
   c) How many times did the devil appeal to Jesus?
      Three
   d) How did Jesus respond each time?
      With the phrase "It is written"
   e) What was He quoting?
      The Word of God

C. CHAPTER HIGHLIGHTS

Before discussing the chapter, define the following:

The War in the Wilderness—the devil's attempt to divert Jesus the Messiah from His divine mission on earth.

Temptation—an enticement to sin, arising from either inner desires or outward circumstances.

Trial—an experience that serves to test or prove the worth of one's character, faith, or holiness; the tests of life that show what we are made of.

Using Chapter Two as background, give a general overview of the chapter. You may want to use the chapter's introduction as a starting point. Be sure to include the following topics:

1. Life Today
2. Types of Temptation
3. After the Temptation
4. Winning the War

II. PART TWO
A. BIBLE STUDY APPLICATION

1. Introduction

   The Bible Study Application section contains 11 questions that provide an opportunity to examine what the Bible says about overcoming temptation and to discuss how we can apply these principles to our lives today.

2. Procedure

Select Small Group Leaders. Ask for volunteers or select five small group leaders. Then assign each small group leader a number from 1-5. (This can also be done beforehand to save time.) Ask the small group leaders to write their numbers on large sheets of white paper so that they can be seen from a distance.

Divide into Small Groups. Inform the participants that they will be separated into five small groups. Each group will study a different set of questions and then will present their findings to the larger group at the end of the study period. The questions should be assigned as follows:

Group #1: The Nature of Temptation (questions 1-4)

Group #2: Examination of Jesus' War in the Wilderness (question 5)

Group #3: Our Spiritual Needs (question 6)

Group #4: Fighting the Battle (questions 7-8)

Group #5: Overcoming: Methods and Rewards (questions 9-11)

Note: If the Bible Study is small, divide into three groups and eliminate discussion groups #2 and #3 (and omit discussion of questions 5 and 6). You may want to assign these as homework.

Allow Participants to Count Off by Fives. Then ask them to follow the small group leader who is holding their assigned number. Identify the location of each group. (These locations can also be pre-printed on a sheet of paper, photocopied, and distributed to save time.) Participants should then assemble into smaller groups in their respective meeting areas.

B. SMALL GROUP STUDY

1. Small Group Leaders

Each group will have one topic to explore. For each topic, there are several questions and related Scripture references to stimulate discussion.

2. Sharing Insights

After 15 minutes, designate someone who will summarize the small group discussion within the larger body of participants. Remind the designated person that she or he will only have two minutes to present.

C. LARGE GROUP PRESENTATIONS

Reconvene the Group. Call the small groups back together.

Explain the Procedure. Explain that a representative of each small group will share that group's reflections on the Bible Study Application questions with the larger group. It may be necessary to pose questions which require them to relate their discussion of Scripture to modern life.

Remind Small Group Representatives of the Time. Remind each group representative that he or she should try to summarize the group's discussion in two minutes. Allow up to two minutes to discuss each group's presentation.

D. LARGE GROUP STUDY*

Personal Application and Church Ministry Discussion. If time permits, the larger group can then discuss the Personal Application and Church Ministry questions together.

1. Introduction

   The Personal Application section contains five questions which encourage participants to consider the teaching in light of their individual circumstances, attitudes, and actions. The Church Ministry section contains three questions which address the implications for congregation as a whole.

2. Sharing Insights

   This discussion should be open-ended and voluntary. The sharing of personal insights or recommendations for church ministry should be encouraged but not required. The group may have quite a bit to say. Watch the clock! Stop them after 10 minutes.

*Answers are not provided for the Personal Application and Church Ministry sections because of the personal or specific nature of the questions.

E. PREPARATION FOR NEXT MEETING

Assignment. Have the participants read Chapter Three, "Hidden in Christ" and review the questions in preparation for next week's session. Encourage them to come to the next session prepared to share their insights on the content of the chapter.

You may also want to assign small groups or questions to facilitate next week's meeting time.

F. CLOSING PRAYER

Hold hands, form a circle, and ask for specific prayer requests. Then ask for several volunteers to pray, keeping the prayer requests in mind.

ANSWERS TO BIBLE STUDY APPLICATION

Passing the Tests of Life

Tests come in various forms. Just as Jesus had to face and overcome trials and temptations in His life, so do we. Our challenge is to meet any attempt to weaken our spirituality in the power of the Holy Spirit.

1. Temptations are common to all of us; no one escapes. What does God promise to do for us when we confront temptation?
   God promises to provide a way of escape.

2. Why was Jesus tempted?
   So that He would be able to help those who are tempted; He can sympathize with us.

3. There is a real hunger in all of us. We often try to fulfill spiritual needs with physical things. What does the Bible say that we are tempted by?
   We are tempted by our own lust or desires.

4. The world will also offer temptations to lure us from our faith in Jesus Christ. What types of satisfaction does the world offer us?
   The lust of the flesh, the lust of the eyes, and the pride of life.

5. The temptations which Jesus faced represent the temptations we face in our own lives. Read the account in Luke 4:1-14 of Jesus' temptation in the wilderness.

   a) In Luke 4:4, what was Jesus' response to the temptation to satisfy the lust of the flesh (gaining food)?

   Man shall not live by bread alone.

   b) What was His response to that same kind of temptation in John 4:34?

   My food is to do the will of Him who sent me, and to accomplish His work.

   c) In Luke 4:8, what was Jesus' response to the temptation to satisfy the lust of the eyes (gaining the kingdoms of the world)?

   You shall worship the Lord your God, and Him only shall you serve.

   d) What was His response to that same kind of temptation in John 18:36?

   My kingdom is not of this world.

   e) In Luke 4:12, what was Jesus' response to the temptation to satisfy the pride of life (exercising His authority over the angels)?

   You shall not tempt the Lord your God.

   f) What was His response to that same kind of temptation in John 6:38?

   For I have come down from heaven, not to do my own will, but the will of Him who sent me.

   g) What was His response to the temptation to walk in darkness or hopelessness in John 8:12?

   I am the light of the world; he who follows me will not walk in darkness, but will have the light of life.

h) In Luke 4:14, how did Jesus leave the encounter in the wilderness to begin His public ministry?

In the power of the Holy Spirit.

6. We will overcome temptation when we recognize that our most important needs are spiritual.

a) What does Jesus say about gaining spiritual food?

Jesus can give living water; Jesus is the bread of life; blessed are they which hunger and thirst after righteousness, for they shall be filled.

b) What does Jesus say about gaining the kingdom of God?

Seek first God's kingdom and His righteousness and all the other things that we need will be added; unless we are born again we cannot see the kingdom of God.

c) What does the Bible say about gaining spiritual authority?

Being humble and child-like is of great value in the kingdom of heaven; Jesus was humble and obedient—we are to be like-minded.

Victory Over Temptation

The war has been won. Jesus won the victory at the Cross; the devil was defeated. However, we are called to walk in victory as overcomers in this life. Jesus overcame the devil by using the same weapons that are available to us today: the Word of God ("It is written"), the power of the Spirit, and prayer.

7. How does the Bible describe the battle against the devil?

Jesus has overcome the world. We can overcome evil
with good. We have the victory through Jesus Christ
our Lord. God always causes us to triumph in Christ.
We have mighty spiritual weapons. We don't wrestle
against flesh and blood. Through His death on the
Cross, Jesus defeated the devil and delivered us from
the fear of death. When we submit to God and resist
the devil, he will flee. Jesus came to destroy the
works of the devil. Greater is He that is in us, than he
that is in the world. Whoever is born of God over-
comes the world; our faith gives us the victory.

8. To be overcomers, we must know how to use our
   weapons. Look up the following Scriptures to see
   how the Bible describes these weapons.
   a) The Word of God

   The Word of God is the sword of the Spirit; it is
   living and active, sharper than any two-edged
   sword, piercing to the division of soul and spirit,
   of joints and marrow, and discerning the thoughts
   and intentions of the heart.
   b) The power of the Holy Spirit

   The Holy Spirit guides us into all truth and shows
   us things to come; gives us the power to become
   witnesses for Jesus; causes us to abound in hope;
   produces mighty signs and wonders; and gives us
   the ability to proclaim Jesus as Lord.
   c) Prayer

   In everything, let your requests be made known to
   God and receive His peace. The prayer of faith
   can save the sick. The effective fervent prayer of
   a righteous man or woman is powerful.

9. What does the Bible say about overcoming the desires of the flesh?

   Put to death sinful habits by the power of the Holy Spirit. Make no provision for the flesh. Continue to live in the Spirit. Be led by the Spirit and not by fleshly desires. Crucify the passions and desires of the flesh, and live according to the will of God.

10. What does the Bible say about overcoming the desires of the mind?

    Love the Lord with all your mind. Set your mind on the things of the Spirit. Renew your mind with the Word of God. Don't be deceived, the wisdom of the world is foolish and futile. Be humble and obedient in attitude and conduct like Jesus. God has given us a sound mind.

11. What rewards are promised to those who overcome?

    The crown of life; permission to eat of the tree of life; protection from the second death; hidden manna and a white stone with a new name written on it; power over nations; white garments and our name in the book of life, announced by Jesus before the Father and the angels; Jesus will make the overcomer a pillar in the temple of God bearing the name of the Lord, the name of the new Jerusalem, and Jesus' own new name; the honor of sitting with Jesus on the throne; a great heritage: He will be our God and we shall be His children.

CHAPTER THREE

HIDDEN IN CHRIST

Lesson format for sessions of 90 minutes or more:

PART ONE		PART TWO	
ACTIVITY	TIME	ACTIVITY	TIME
Opening Prayer	5 min.	Small Group Study	20 min.
Scripture Reading	5 min.	Large Group Presentations	20 min.
Scripture Search	5 min.	Large Group Discussion	10 min.
Chapter Highlights	20 min.	Closing Prayer	5 min.

For sessions of less than 90 minutes, use PART ONE only and assign the Bible Study Application section as homework.

LESSON AIMS: At the end of this two-part session, the participant should be able to: a) discuss the sufficiency of God's saving grace; b) distinguish between the old "I" and the new "I"; c) define what it means for the Christian to live "in Christ."

I. PART ONE

A. OPENING PRAYER

Open the session with prayer. Include the request that each participant would receive the following:

- A clearer understanding of the significance of Jesus' finished work on the Cross.
- Greater insight into why we must be born again.
- An increased awareness of the freedom and power available to those who live in Christ.

B. SCRIPTURE SEARCH

1. Ask someone to read Galatians 2:15-21 aloud to the group.
2. Clarify the context of this passage by explaining the following:

   The Jews were considered to be the people of God (Hebrews 8:10). For them, keeping the laws of God was a serious part of their religious heritage and tradition.

3. Ask for volunteers to answer the following questions:

   a) How are we justified (declared righteous)?

   We are justified by our faith in Jesus Christ.

   b) Can we be justified by keeping the Ten Commandments or by our own good behavior?

   No, we are justified by our faith in Jesus Christ alone.

   c) In your own words, what does it mean to be crucified with Christ?

   Answers will vary. If needed, read Romans 6:6 to clarify.

   d) In your own words, what does it mean to live by

faith in the Son of God?
Answers will vary. If needed, read Romans 1:7
and Hebrews 10:38 to clarify.

C. CHAPTER HIGHLIGHTS

Before discussing the chapter, define the following:

The Lost "I" — the complete surrender of one's life to the control of Jesus Christ.

Exchanging the old "I" for the new "I" — moving from self-centeredness to Christ-centeredness; or moving from the self-life to the life of Christ, or the truly Christian life.

Using Chapter Three as background, give a general overview of the chapter. You may want to use the chapter's introduction as a starting point. Be sure to include the following topics:

1. The Lost "I"
2. Time for a Trade-in
3. New and Free
4. New and Power-filled
5. Living in Christ

II. PART TWO
A. BIBLE STUDY APPLICATION

1. Introduction

    The Bible Study Application section contains 10 questions that provide an opportunity to examine what the Bible says about living the Christian life and to discuss how these truths should be demonstrated in our lives today.

2. Procedure

Select Small Group Leaders. Ask for volunteers or select three small group leaders. Then assign each small group leader a number from 1-3. (This can be done beforehand to save time.) Ask the small group leaders to write their numbers on large sheets of white paper so that they can be seen from a distance.

Divide into Small Groups. Inform the participants that they will be separated into three small groups. Each group will study a different set of questions and then will present their findings to the larger group at the end of the study period. The questions should be assigned as follows:

> Group #1: What's Wrong with the Old "I"? (questions 1-4)
>
> Group #2: What Happened to the Old Life? (questions 5-7)
>
> Group #3: Our New Life in Christ (questions 6-10)

Allow Participants to Count Off by Threes. Then ask them to follow the small group leader who is holding their assigned number. Identify the location of each group. (These locations can be pre-printed on a sheet of paper, photocopied, and distributed to save time.) Participants should then assemble into smaller groups in their respective meeting areas.

B. SMALL GROUP STUDY
1. Small Group Leaders

    Each group will have one topic to explore. For each topic, there are several questions and related

Scripture references to stimulate discussion.

2. Sharing Insights
   After 15 minutes, designate someone who will summarize the small group discussion within the larger body of participants. Remind the designated person that she or he will only have two minutes to present.

C. LARGE GROUP PRESENTATIONS
Reconvene the Group. Call the small groups back together.

Explain the Procedure. Explain that a representative of each small group will share that group's reflections on the Bible Study Application questions with the larger group. It may be necessary to pose questions which require them to relate their discussion of Scripture to modern life.

Remind Small Group Representatives of the Time. Remind each group representative that he or she should try to summarize the group's discussion in two minutes. Allow up to two minutes to discuss each group's presentation.

D. LARGE GROUP STUDY*
Personal Application and Church Ministry Discussion. If time permits, the larger group can then discuss the Personal Application and Church Ministry questions together.

1. Introduction

The Personal Application section contains five questions which encourage the participants to consider the teaching in light of their own lives. The Church Ministry section contains three questions which address some implications for the congregation as a whole.

2. Sharing Insights

This discussion should be open-ended and voluntary. The sharing of personal insights or recommendations for church ministry should be encouraged but not required. The group may have quite a bit to say. Watch the clock! Stop them after 10 minutes.

*Answers are not provided for the Personal Application and Church Ministry sections because of the personal or specific nature of the questions.

E. PREPARATION FOR NEXT MEETING

Assignment. Have the participants read Chapter Four, "Power from on High" and review the questions in preparation for next week's session. Encourage them to come to the next session prepared to share their insights on the content of the chapter.

You may also want to assign small groups or questions to facilitate next week's meeting time.

F. CLOSING PRAYER

Hold hands, form a circle, and ask for specific prayer requests. Then ask for several volunteers to pray, keeping the prayer requests in mind.

ANSWERS TO BIBLE STUDY

APPLICATION

Being Hidden in Christ
In order to enjoy the fullness of Christian living, we must unite ourselves totally with Christ; we must allow ourselves to be lost in Him. Our identification with Christ comes from the surrender of our lives to Him and not from our good works. We must die to ourselves and allow the Holy Spirit to fill our lives.

1. Read Isaiah 53:4-11. Use these verses to answer the following questions.
   a) What's wrong with the old "I"?
      The old "I" has turned from the way of God to go its own way (v. 6).
   b) Why did Christ die for us?
      Jesus took our sins and bore our punishment (vv. 5-6) and in exchange offers us righteousness through knowing Him (v. 11).

2. Read Romans 1:18-32. Use these verses to answer the following questions.
   a) What's wrong with the old "I"?
      The old "I" does not honor God as God or give Him thanks (v. 21). Since the old "I" does not acknowledge God, God has removed His restraint and protection of the mind. Therefore, the old "I" enjoys evil and even encourages the sinful practices of others (vv. 28-32).
   b) Why are we "without excuse"?
      From the beginning of creation, the heavens and the earth declare and testify to the eternal power

and divinity of God (v. 20).

3. Read Romans 3:10-20. Use these verses to answer the following questions.
   a) What's wrong with the old "I"?
      The old "I" is unrighteous (v. 10), without under-standing and does not seek God (v. 11), has turned aside and become worthless (v. 12), does not show kindness, participates in evil speaking and activities (vv. 13-17), and does not fear God (v. 18).
   b) Are some of us better than others in the sight of God?
      No one is righteous, not even one (v. 10). No human being will be justified in His sight (v. 20).

4. Read Romans 3:21-26. Use these verses to answer the following questions.
   a) What's wrong with the old "I"?
      The old "I" has sinned and falls short of the glory of God (v. 23).
   b) Are we justified by the Law or by grace?
      We are justified by grace as a gift through the redemption that is in Christ Jesus (v. 20).

5. Read Romans 6:3-11. Use these verses to answer the following questions.
   a) What has happened to your old life?
      It has been buried with Christ; the death of the old life is symbolized by baptism (vv. 3-4).
   b) What have we been made free from?

We have been made free from the power of sin (vv. 6-7).

c) What have we been made alive to?

We have been made alive to God in Jesus Christ (v. 11).

6. Read 2 Corinthians 5:14-21. Use these verses to answer the following questions.

   a) What has happened to your old life?

   It has passed away (v. 17).

   b) How do we receive new life?

   It comes from God as a result of our being in (belonging to) Christ (vv. 17-18).

7. Read Galatians 2:19-20. Use these verses to answer the following questions.

   a) What has happened to your old life?

   It is dead—crucified with Christ (v. 19).

   b) How do we live the new life?

   By faith in the Son of God (v. 20).

8. Read Ephesians 2:4-10. Use these verses to answer the following questions.

   a) How have we been made "alive together with Christ"?

   By God's grace (vv. 5, 8).

   b) Why can't a Christian ever truthfully say that he or she is a self-made man or woman?

   Grace is a gift of God. It is not the result of works, so no one can boast (vv. 8-9).

c) Once we have accepted God's gift of salvation, how should this truth affect the way we live?

Since we have been created in Christ Jesus for good works, we should show them in our conduct, our attitudes, and our lifestyle (v. 10).

9. Read Colossians 3:1-4. Use these verses to answer the following questions.

   a) How does our new life affect our goals?

   We should seek the things that are above in heaven (v. 1).

   b) How does our new life affect our thoughts?

   We should set our minds on the things that are in heaven (v. 2).

   c) How does our new life affect our expected rewards?

   We should expect heavenly rewards (v. 4).

10. Read the words of Jesus in Mark 8:35. Explain what this verse means in light of Paul's teachings about our life in Christ.

   As we surrender (or lose) our old life for Christ's sake and the sake of the Gospel, we will gain the life of Christ and salvation in Him.

CHAPTER FOUR

POWER FROM ON HIGH

Lesson format for sessions of 90 minutes or more:

PART ONE		PART TWO	
ACTIVITY	TIME	ACTIVITY	TIME
Opening Prayer	5 min.	Small Group Study	20 min.
Scripture Reading	5 min.	Large Group Presentations	20 min.
Scripture Search	5 min.	Large Group Discussion	10 min.
Chapter Highlights	20 min.	Closing Prayer	5 min.

For sessions of less than 90 minutes, use PART ONE only and assign the Bible Study Application section as homework.

LESSON AIMS: At the end of this two-part session, the participant should be able to: a) distinguish between natural (physical) power and spiritual power; b) identify the benefits of waiting on God; c) understand the importance of unity; d) describe the role of the Holy Spirit in the life of the believer.

I. PART ONE
A. OPENING PRAYER

Open the session with prayer. Include the request that each participant would receive the following:

- A greater understanding of why we need spiritual power.
- An increased awareness of power of the Holy Spirit.
- A greater desire to see the power of the Holy Spirit demonstrated in our lives.

B. SCRIPTURE SEARCH

1. Ask someone to read Acts 1:3-9 and 2:1-4 aloud to the group.
2. Ask for volunteers to answer the following questions:
   a) What is Jesus referring to when He mentions the "gift my Father promised"?

   The gift that God promised was the power of the Holy Spirit.

   b) What kind of kingdom were the disciples looking for Jesus to establish?

   They thought that Jesus would establish an earthly kingdom.

   c) What kind of power was Jesus telling them to wait for?

   Jesus told them to wait for supernatural power which they would receive in the form of the Holy Spirit.

   d) Why do you think Jesus uses the term "receive"?
   The Holy Spirit is a gift from God.

   e) What else does the Bible say that we receive as a gift from God?

Eternal life is a gift from God.

f) What power did the disciples receive on the Day of Pentecost?

They received the power to be witnesses for Jesus Christ.

g) What were the results of their power-filled witness about the identity and the work of Jesus Christ? (Acts 2:37, 41)

People were cut to their hearts, and 3000 people became believers in Jesus Christ and were added to the Church that day.

C. CHAPTER HIGHLIGHTS

Using Chapter Four as background, give a general overview of the chapter. You may want to use the introduction as a starting point. Be sure to include the following topics:

1. The Power to Make a Difference
2. Waiting for the Promise
3. The Importance of Unity
4. The Work of the Spirit
5. Filled and Speaking the Language
6. When the Spirit Comes

II. PART TWO
A. BIBLE STUDY APPLICATION

1. Introduction

The Bible Study Application section contains 10 questions that provide an opportunity to examine what the Bible says about the power of the Holy Spirit.

2. Procedure

Select Small Group Leaders. Ask for volunteers or select three small group leaders. Then assign each small group leader a number from 1-3. (This can be done beforehand to save time.) Ask the small group leaders to write their numbers on large sheets of white paper so that they can be seen from a distance.

Divide into Small Groups. Inform the participants that they will be separated into three small groups. Each group will study a different set of questions and then will present their findings to the larger group at the end of the study period. The questions should be assigned as follows:

Group #1: Heirs of the Kingdom (questions 1-4)
Group #2: Possessors of Power (questions 5-7)
Group #3: Witnesses for Jesus (questions 8-10)

Allow Participants to Count Off by Threes. Then ask them to follow the small group leader who is holding their assigned number. Identify the location of each group. (These locations can also be pre-printed on a sheet of paper, photocopied, and distributed to save time.) Participants should then assemble into smaller groups in their respective meeting areas.

B. SMALL GROUP STUDY

1. Small Group Leaders

Each group will have one topic to explore. For each topic, there are several questions and related Scripture references to stimulate discussion.

2. Sharing Insights
   After 15 minutes, designate someone who will sum-marize the small group discussion within the larger body of participants. Remind the designated person about the two-minute time limit.

C. LARGE GROUP PRESENTATIONS
Reconvene the Group. Call the small groups back together.

Explain the Procedure. Explain that a representative of each small group will share that group's reflections on the Bible Study Application questions with the larg-er group. It may be necessary to pose questions which require them to relate their discussion of Scripture to modern life.

Remind Small Group Representatives of the Time. Remind each group representative that he or she should try to summarize the group's discussion in two minutes. Allow up to two minutes to discuss each group's pre-sentation.

D. LARGE GROUP STUDY*
Personal Application and Church Ministry Discussion. If time permits, the larger group can then discuss the Personal Application and Church Ministry questions together.

1. Introduction
   The Personal Application section contains five ques-tions which encourage the participants to consider the teaching in light of their own lives. The Church

Ministry section contains three questions which address the implications for the congregation as a whole.

2. Sharing Insights

This discussion should be open-ended and voluntary. The sharing of personal insights or recommendations for church ministry should be encouraged but not required. The group may have quite a bit to say. Watch the clock! Stop them after 10 minutes.

*Answers are not provided for the Personal Application or Church Ministry sections because of the personal or specific nature of the questions.

E. PREPARATION FOR NEXT MEETING

Assignment. Have the participants read Chapter Five, "The Purpose of Prayer" and review the questions in preparation for next week's session. Encourage them to come to the next session prepared to share their insights on the content of the chapter.

You may also want to assign small groups or questions to facilitate next week's meeting time.

F. CLOSING PRAYER

Hold hands, form a circle, ask for specific prayer requests. Then ask for several volunteers to pray, keeping the prayer requests in mind.

ANSWERS TO BIBLE STUDY APPLICATION

Heirs of the Kingdom

Jesus' method of establishing the kingdom of God was not based on changing the existing political, economic, or social structure. It was based on changing the human heart by the power of the Holy Spirit.

1. Use the verses in parentheses to answer the following questions concerning the nature of God's Kingdom.
   a) Describe the characteristics of the kingdom of God.

   The kingdom of God is not found in natural (physical) things but in spiritual things.
   b) Where is the kingdom of God?

   The kingdom of God is inside of believers.
   c) How do we enter the kingdom of God?

   We enter God's kingdom by becoming born again.

2. Match the following verses to their description of the coming of the Holy Spirit.

   b. Clothed with power from on high

   c. Baptized with the Holy Spirit and with fire

   a. Poured out on all flesh

3. Use the following verses to describe how the Holy Spirit was sent to believers.
   a) In whose name or under whose authority was the Holy Spirit sent to believers?

   The Holy Spirit was sent in the name of Jesus.

b) From where did the Holy Spirit come?
The Holy came from the Father.

4. Read Romans 8:14-17. Use these verses to describe how we know that we are the children of God.
a) We have the Holy Spirit.
b) We are led by the Spirit.
c) We have the inner witness of the Spirit.

Possessors of Power
The disciples waited in Jerusalem for the promised Holy Spirit. Today, the power of Holy Spirit is available to every believer.

5. The Holy Spirit is called the "promise of the Father." Use the verses in parentheses to answer the following questions about receiving God's promise.
a) To whom is the Holy Spirit promised?
The Holy Spirit is for all who are called to salvation.
b) How do we receive the Holy Spirit?
We receive the promise of the Holy Spirit through faith in Jesus Christ.
c) When do we receive the Holy Spirit?
After we have believed the Gospel and received the gift of salvation through Jesus Christ.
d) How can we identify the Holy Spirit?
The Holy Spirit always glorifies and reveals Jesus Christ.
e) How long will the Holy Spirit abide with us?
He will be with us forever.

6. Describe the work of the Holy Spirit in the life of the believer.

   a) He sanctifies and justifies us.

   b) He dwells with us.

   c) He leads us.

   d) He strengthens our inner selves.

   e) He enables us to speak with authority.

   f) He helps us pray and He prays for us.

   g) He makes us abound in hope.

7. Use the following verses to identify other ways that the power of the Holy Spirit is exhibited.

   a) In creation

   b) In the conception of Christ

   c) In the working of miracles

   d) In the resurrection of Jesus Christ

Witnesses for Jesus

A witness is one who tells what he or she has heard, seen, or experienced. It is the power of the Holy Spirit which makes our witness for Jesus Christ effective in the lives of others.

8. As believers in Christ, we are called to share the Gospel. What is the Gospel?

   The Gospel is the good news that Christ died for our sins in accordance with the Scriptures; that He was buried, and that He was raised on the third day in accordance with the Scriptures.

9. Use the following verses to describe how the Holy Spirit empowers our witness.

a) He opens the hearts of men and women.

b) He convicts the world of sin.

c) He reveals the truth about Jesus Christ.

d) He empowers the Gospel.

10. We can learn much from the account of Jesus witnessing to the woman of Samaria. Read John 4:4-30, 39-42. Identify which verse(s) shows that:

a) Jesus "spoke her language" and opened the conversation on a subject that was familiar to her.
Verse 7

b) He turned the conversation from natural things to spiritual things.
Verse 10

c) He brought her to recognize the fact of her sin.
Verse 16

d) He revealed Himself as Christ.
Verse 26

e) His witness produced results. She became a believer and brought others to Christ.
Verses 39-42

CHAPTER FIVE

THE PURPOSE OF PRAYER

Lesson format for sessions of 90 minutes or more:

PART ONE		PART TWO	
ACTIVITY	TIME	ACTIVITY	TIME
Opening Prayer	5 min.	Small Group Study	20 min.
Scripture Reading	5 min.	Large Group Presentations	20 min.
Scripture Search	5 min.	Large Group Discussion	10 min.
Chapter Highlights	20 min.	Closing Prayer	5 min.

For sessions of less than 90 minutes, use PART ONE only and assign the Bible Study Application section as homework.

LESSON AIMS: At the end of this two-part session, the participant should be able to: a) recognize the role of private prayer in the spiritual life of the believer; b) distinguish between different types of prayer; c) describe what happens when we communicate with God in prayer.

I. PART ONE
A. OPENING PRAYER

Open the session with prayer. Include the request that each participant would receive the following:

- A greater understanding of why we need to pray.
- An increased awareness of what God does for us and in us when we meet with Him in prayer.

B. SCRIPTURE SEARCH

1. Ask someone to read Mark 1:32-39 aloud to the group.
2. Ask for volunteers to answer the following questions:

   a) What time did Jesus choose to pray?

   Early in the morning, while it was still dark.

   b) Why do you think He chose that time to be alone and communicate with God?

   Answers will vary. However, the busier we are, the more important it is that we make time to get away and get alone in the presence of God.

   c) What did the disciples do while Jesus prayed?

   They woke up and began to search for Him. Our responsibilities will often track us down.

   d) When they found Him, how did His answer show that He had received direction from God?

   He answered that they should go on to the neighboring towns so that He could continue the work of God.

   e) What was the evidence that Jesus had received power in prayer?

   He went throughout Galilee, proclaiming the message and casting out demons.

C. CHAPTER HIGHLIGHTS

Using Chapter Five as background, give a general overview of the chapter. You may want to use the chapter's introduction as a starting point. Be sure to include the following topics:

1. The Demands of Life
2. The Example of Our Lord
3. What Is Prayer?
4. What Happens in Prayer?

II. PART TWO
A. BIBLE STUDY APPLICATION

1. Introduction

   The Bible Study Application section contains 10 questions that provide an opportunity to examine what the Bible says about the importance of private prayer, and to discuss how the principles and privileges of prayer can be applied to our lives today.

2. Procedure

   Select Small Group Leaders. Ask for volunteers or select four small group leaders. Then assign each small group leader a number from 1-4. (This can be done beforehand to save time.) Ask the small group leaders to write their numbers on large sheets of white paper so that they can be seen from a distance.

   Divide into Small Groups. Inform the participants that they will be separated into four small groups. Each group will study a different set of questions and then will present their findings to the larger group at the end of the study period. The questions should be assigned as follows:

Group #1: Private Prayer Is Essential (questions 1-3)

Group #2: The Lord's Prayer (question 4)

Group #3: The Principles and Privileges of Prayer; Part 1 (questions 5-8)

Group #4: The Principles and Privileges of Prayer; Part 2 (questions 9-10)

Allow Participants to Count Off by Fours. Then ask them to follow the small group leader who is holding their assigned number. Identify the location of each group. (These locations can be pre-printed on a sheet of paper, photocopied, and distributed to save time.) Participants should then assemble into smaller groups in their respective meeting areas.

B. SMALL GROUP STUDY
1. Small Group Leaders

   Each group will have one topic to explore. For each topic, there are several questions and related Scripture references to stimulate discussion.

2. Sharing Insights

   After 15 minutes, designate someone who will summarize the small group discussion within the larger body of participants. Remind the designated person that she or he will only have two minutes to present.

C. LARGE GROUP PRESENTATIONS
Reconvene the Group. Call the small groups back together.

Explain the Procedure. Explain that a representative

of each small group will share that group's reflections on the Bible Study Application questions with the larger group. It may be necessary to pose questions which require them to relate their discussion of Scripture to modern life.

Remind Small Group Representatives of the Time. Remind each group representative that he or she should try to summarize the group's discussion in two minutes. Allow up to two minutes to discuss each group's presentation.

D. LARGE GROUP STUDY*

Personal Application and Church Ministry Discussion. If time permits, the larger group can then discuss the Personal Application and Church Ministry questions together.

1. Introduction

   The Personal Application section contains five questions which encourage participants to consider the teaching in light of their own lives. The Church Ministry section contains three questions which address the implications for the congregation as a whole.

2. Sharing Insights

   This discussion should be open-ended and voluntary. The sharing of personal insights or recommendations for church ministry should be encouraged but not required. The group may have quite a bit to say. Watch the clock! Stop them after 10 minutes.

*Answers are not provided for the Personal Application and Church Ministry sections because of the personal or specific nature of the questions.

E. PREPARATION FOR NEXT MEETING
Assignment. Have the participants read Chapter Six, "The Reason We Sing" and review the questions in preparation for next week's session. Encourage them to come to the next session prepared to share their insights on the content of the chapter.

You may also want to assign small groups or questions to facilitate next week's meeting time.

F. CLOSING PRAYER
Hold hands, form a circle, and ask for specific prayer requests. Then ask for several volunteers to pray, keeping the prayer requests in mind.

ANSWERS TO BIBLE STUDY APPLICATION

Private Prayer Is Essential
Public prayer is necessary in the life of the church. Praying together as a family is necessary for the strength of the home. But private prayer is essential to the spiritual life of the individual.

1. In Matthew 6:5, what does Jesus say about those who pray to be seen of men?
   Jesus calls them hypocrites and says that they have their reward—the earthly, fleeting attention or admiration of men.

2. In Matthew 6:6, what does Jesus say about those who pray to the Father in secret?
The Father shall reward them openly; they will receive a heavenly reward that can be plainly recognized.

3. In Matthew 6:7-8, what does Jesus say about those who use vain repetitions in prayer (repeating the same prayer or saying the same phrases and words over and over again)?
Jesus calls them heathens and admonishes us not to be like them. It is not how we ask or how much we say in prayer that matters. God already knows our needs and He knows our hearts. We must be sincere with God.

The Lord's Prayer
Although commonly referred to as "The Lord's Prayer," Jesus' prayer in Matthew 6:9-13 is really a model for prayer that He gave to the disciples. Jesus was not telling the disciples to pray this prayer word for word. He was giving a pattern or set of principles for prayer that we can follow today.

4. Read Matthew 6:9-13. Match the following phrases with the principles that they illustrate.
   d. Our Father which art in heaven
   b. Hallowed be thy name
   a. Thy kingdom come, thy will be done on earth as it is in heaven
   e. Give us this day our daily bread
   c. And forgive us for our debts

h. As we forgive our debtors

g. And lead us not into temptation, but deliver us from evil

f. For thine is the kingdom, and the power, and the glory, forever. Amen.

The Principles and Privileges of Prayer

Some may regard prayer as a burdensome responsibility, when in fact it is a priceless privilege. As we follow the principles of the Word of God and the leading of the Holy Spirit, we will experience the benefits of answered prayer.

5. What does Matthew 7:11 say about the privilege of knowing God as our Father?

God loves us and wants us to have good things, just as we love our children and want them to have good things.

6. What does Psalm 100:4 say about the principle of praise?

That we are to enter into the presence of God with thanksgiving and praise.

7. What does Matthew 6:33 say about the principle of putting God first?

If we seek first the kingdom of God and His righteousness, all the other things that we need will be provided for us as well.

8. What does Matthew 18:21-35 say about the principle of forgiveness?

We are to forgive others because God has forgiven us.

9. Read Philippians 4:6-7. Use these verses to answer the following questions.

   a) What are we to worry about?

   Nothing.

   b) What are we to pray about?

   Everything.

   c) What is prayer?

   Prayer is communication with God.

   d) What is supplication?

   Supplication is asking God to supply our needs.

   e) Why should we give thanks when we pray?

   By giving thanks before we see the result, we demonstrate our confidence and faith in God's ability to answer and work on our behalf.

   g) If we refuse to worry and instead we pray about everything, what will we receive as a result?

   We will receive the peace of God.

10. Why can we be confident in God's supply?

   God's Word gives us confidence in Him. He says that He will supply all our needs and He has inexhaustible resources.

CHAPTER SIX

THE REASON
WE SING

Lesson format for sessions of 90 minutes or more:

PART ONE		PART TWO	
ACTIVITY	TIME	ACTIVITY	TIME
Opening Prayer	5 min.	Small Group Study	20 min.
Scripture Reading	5 min.	Large Group Presentations	20 min.
Scripture Search	5 min.	Large Group Discussion	10 min.
Chapter Highlights	20 min.	Closing Prayer	5 min.

For sessions of less than 90 minutes, use PART ONE only and assign the Bible Study Application section as homework.

LESSON AIMS: At the end of this two-part session, the participant should be able to: a) describe the importance of musical expression in the spiritual life of the believer; b) explain why we should sing a new song to the Lord; c) identify the types of songs that believers can sing.

I. PART ONE
A. OPENING PRAYER

Open the session with prayer. Include the request that each participant would receive the following:

- An increased awareness of the power of praise.
- A greater understanding of how the music of the Church helps us understand the work and will of God.
- A greater desire to sing new songs as we lift our hearts and souls to God.

B. SCRIPTURE SEARCH

1. Ask someone to read Psalm 96:1-9 aloud to the group.
2. Ask for volunteers to answer the following questions:
   a) What does Psalm 96 encourage believers to do?
      To sing a new song to the Lord.
   b) What name should we praise in song?
      We should praise the name of the Lord.
   c) What should we proclaim in song?
      We should proclaim the salvation of the Lord every day.
   d) What should we declare in song?
      We should declare God's glory among the nations and His marvelous deeds among the people.
   e) What kind of new song does Psalm 96 encourage us to sing?
      We are encouraged to sing a new song of praise to God.

C. CHAPTER HIGHLIGHTS

Using Chapter Six as background, give a general

overview of the chapter. You may want to use the introduction as a starting point. Be sure to include the following topics:

1. Today's Music
2. The Good Old Songs
3. A New Song for a New Day
4. The Song of Joy
5. The Song of Salvation
6. The Song of Praise
7. The Song of the Redeemed
8. Singing from the Heart

II. PART TWO
A. BIBLE STUDY APPLICATION

1. Introduction

The Bible Study Application section contains 11 questions that provide an opportunity to examine what the Bible says about the effect of singing praises to God, the value of singing new songs to the Lord, and the importance of singing heartfelt songs to God.

2. Procedure

Select Small Group Leaders. Ask for volunteers or select four small group leaders. Then assign each small group leader a number from 1-4. (This can be done beforehand to save time.) Ask the small group leaders to write their numbers on large sheets of white paper so that they can be seen from a distance.

Divide into Small Groups. Inform the participants that they will be separated into four small groups. Each group will study a different set of questions and

73

then will present their findings to the larger group at the end of the study period. The questions should be assigned as follows:

Group #1: The Power of Praise (questions 1-3)

Group #2: Singing a New Song (question 4)

Group #3: Songs from the Heart (questions 5-6)

Group #4: On Earth as in Heaven (questions 7-11)

Allow Participants to Count Off by Fours. Then ask them to follow the small group leader who is holding their assigned number. Identify the location of each group. (These locations can be pre-printed on a sheet of paper, photocopied, and distributed to save time.) Participants should then assemble into smaller groups in their respective meeting areas.

B. SMALL GROUP STUDY

1. Small Group Leaders

Each group will have one topic to explore. For each topic, there are several questions and related Scripture references to stimulate discussion.

2. Sharing Insights

After 15 minutes, designate someone who will summarize the small group discussion within the larger body of participants. Remind the designated person that she or he will only have two minutes to present.

C. LARGE GROUP PRESENTATIONS

Reconvene the Group. Call the small groups back together.

Explain the Procedure. Explain that a representative

of each small group will share that group's reflections on the Bible Study Application questions with the larger group. It may be necessary to pose questions which require them to relate their discussion of Scripture to modern life.

Remind Small Group Representatives of the Time. Remind each group representative that he or she should try to summarize the group's discussion in two minutes. Allow up to two minutes to discuss each group's presentation.

D. LARGE GROUP STUDY*
Personal Application and Church Ministry Discussion. If time permits, the larger group can then discuss the Personal Application and Church Ministry questions together.

1. Introduction
   The Personal Application section contains five questions which encourage the participants to consider the teaching in light of their own lives. The Church Ministry section contains three questions which address some implications for the congregation as a whole.

2. Sharing Insights
   This discussion should be open-ended and voluntary. The sharing of personal insights or recommendations for church ministry should be encouraged but not required. The group may have quite a bit to say. Watch the clock! Stop them after 10 minutes.

*Answers are not provided for the Personal Application

and Church Ministry sections because of the personal or specific nature of the questions.

E. PREPARATION FOR NEXT MEETING

Assignment. Have the participants read Chapter Seven, "Living in the Spirit" and review the questions in preparation for next week's session. Encourage them to come to the next session prepared to share their insights on the content of the chapter.

You may also want to assign small groups or questions to facilitate next week's meeting time.

F. CLOSING PRAYER

Hold hands, form a circle, and ask for specific prayer requests. Then ask for several volunteers to pray, keeping the prayer requests in mind.

ANSWERS TO BIBLE STUDY APPLICATION

The Power of Praise

Like prayer, music is a powerful form of communication. In fact, musical lyrics can be viewed as speech intensified. As we worship and praise God in song, the music which results can change the atmosphere as well as the attitude of the heart.

1. Read 1 Samuel 16:14-16, 23. Use these verses to answer the following questions.
   a) Who was the musician?
   David.
   b) For whom was he playing?

Saul.

c) What type of music was played?

David played on his harp.

d) What effect did the music have?

The music caused Saul to become refreshed and well, and the evil spirit left Saul.

2. Read 2 Chronicles 20:20-22. Use these verses to answer the following questions.

a) Who were the singers?

The people of Judah and Jerusalem who were appointed by Jehoshaphat to march ahead of the army.

b) To whom were they singing?

The Lord.

c) What type of song was sung?

They sang a song of praise and thanksgiving.

d) What happened when they began to sing?

The Lord set ambushes against their enemies so that their enemies were utterly destroyed.

3. Read Acts 16:25-26. Use these verses to answer the following questions.

a) Who were the singers?

Paul and Silas.

b) To whom were they singing?

They were singing to God.

c) What type of song did they sing?

They sang hymns.

d) What happened while they prayed and sang?

Suddenly there was an earthquake, and the doors

of the prison were opened and everyone's chains were unfastened.

Singing a New Song

We have become new creatures in Christ (2 Corinthians 5:17). Through Christ, we have been given access to God by "a new and living way" (Hebrews 10:20). Each day we face new circumstances. As we obey God, we will experience His power, provision, and protection in new ways. It is no wonder that Scripture repeatedly exhorts us to sing a new song to the Lord.

4. Match the following Scripture references with the reasons that we should sing a new song.

c. For God has done marvelous things.

a. For the Word of the Lord is upright, and all His work is done in faithfulness.

b. For great is the Lord and greatly to be praised.

d. For God gives victory to kings and rescues His servant.

e. For the Lord takes pleasure in His people, and He adorns the humble with victory.

f. For the Lord shows Himself mighty against His foes.

Songs from the Heart

Music is an important form of human expression, but there is a difference between a good performance, excellent entertainment, and heartfelt praise. The music of the Church must be different. As believers in Christ, we are a chosen people, a royal priesthood, a holy nation, and a people who belong to God. Therefore, we must declare the praises of Him who has called us out of darkness into His wonderful light (1 Peter 2:9).

5. Read Ephesians 5:19 and Colossians 3:16. Use these verses to answer to the following questions.
    a) What are three ways that we are encouraged to speak or sing?
       We are to speak or sing psalms, hymns, and spiritual songs.
    b) Where should the songs and the melody come from?
       We are to sing and make melody to the Lord from our hearts.
    c) What type of attitude should we have when we sing to God?
       We are to sing to God with gratitude in our hearts.

6. Read Matthew 15:8 and John 4:23-24. Describe the importance of singing to God from our hearts.
   God is not honored by lip service. We must sing to Him from our hearts and worship Him in spirit and in truth.

On Earth as in Heaven
We often sing and pray, "Thy will be done on earth as it is in heaven." In the Book of Revelation, we get a glimpse of the fervent, new songs of praise that ring throughout heaven.

7. Read Revelation 5:8-9. Use these verses to answer the following questions.
    a) Who were the singers?
       The four living creatures and the 24 elders.
    b) To whom were they singing?

The Lamb of God (the Lord Jesus Christ).

c) What type of song did they sing?

They sang a new song of praise.

8. Read Revelation 5:11-12. Use these verses to answer the following questions.

    a) Who were the singers?

    Myriads and myriads (10,000 times 10,000) and (plus) thousands of thousands of angels.

    b) How were they singing?

    They were singing in full voice.

    c) To whom were they singing?

    The Lamb of God (the Lord Jesus Christ).

    d) What type of song did they sing?

    They sang a song of praise.

9. Read Revelation 5:13-14. Use these verses to answer the following questions.

    a) Who were the singers?

    Every creature in heaven, and on earth, and under the earth, and in the sea, and all that is in them.

    b) To whom were they singing?

    To the One who sits on the throne and to the Lamb (or to the Lord our God and to the Lord Jesus Christ).

    c) What type of song did they sing?

    They sang a song of praise.

10. Read Revelation 14:1-3. Use these verses to answer

the following questions.

a) Who were the singers?

One hundred and forty-four thousand people who had the name of the Lamb and the Father written on their foreheads. They were the ones who had been redeemed from the earth.

b) What type of song did they sing?

They sang a new song that only they could learn.

c) Where did they sing their song?

They sang before the throne of God and before the four living creatures and before the elders.

11. Read Revelation 15:2-3. Use these verses to answer the following questions.

a) Who were the singers?

Those who had conquered the beast and its image and the number of its name.

b) What instrument were they holding?

They held harps of God in their hands.

c) What type of song did they sing?

They sang the song of Moses—a song of praise after God has provided deliverance and victory.

d) To whom were they singing?

They sang to the Lord, the Almighty God.

CHAPTER SEVEN

LIVING IN THE SPIRIT

Lesson format for sessions of 90 minutes or more:

PART ONE		PART TWO	
ACTIVITY	TIME	ACTIVITY	TIME
Opening Prayer	5 min.	Small Group Study	20 min.
Scripture Reading	5 min.	Large Group Presentations	20 min.
Scripture Search	5 min.	Large Group Discussion	10 min.
Chapter Highlights	20 min.	Closing Prayer	5 min.

For sessions of less than 90 minutes, use PART ONE only and assign the Bible Study Application section as homework.

LESSON AIMS: At the end of this two-part session, the participant should be able to: a) identify the power for living the Christian life; b) explain how we can live in the Spirit; c) describe the results of living in the Spirit.

I. PART ONE
A. OPENING PRAYER

Open the session with prayer. Include the request that each participant would receive the following:

- An increased awareness of the power that God makes available to us through the Holy Spirit.
- A greater understanding of how we can live in the Spirit.

B. SCRIPTURE SEARCH

1. Ask someone to read Romans 8:1-8 aloud to the group.
2. Ask for volunteers to answer the following questions:

   a) Who has escaped condemnation?

   There is now no condemnation for those who are in Christ Jesus.

   b) What have we been set free from?

   The law of the Spirit of life has set us free from the law of sin and death.

   c) Who was sent to be a sin offering for us? (See also 2 Corinthians 5:21.)

   God sent His own Son, Jesus Christ, into the world in human form to be a sin offering for us. Jesus, who was without sin, became sin for us, so that the righteousness of God might be made available to us in Him.

   d) Read Romans 8:5. What two groups of people are described in this verse?

   This passage of Scripture describes those who live according to the Spirit and those who live according to the sinful nature or the flesh.

   e) As we live according to the Spirit, what changes?

As we live according to the Spirit, our mind set changes. Instead of natural desires, our minds are set on what the Spirit desires. Instead of producing death, our mind set produces life and peace.

C. CHAPTER HIGHLIGHTS

Before discussing the chapter, define the following:

The law of the Spirit of life — the controlling power of the Holy Spirit operating in the hearts of believers as they commit themselves to obey the Word of God and the leading of the Holy Spirit.

The law of sin and death — the controlling power of sin which places people in bondage and results in death.

Living in the Spirit — to be under the control of the Holy Spirit, living in accordance with what He wants.

Using Chapter Seven as background, give a general overview of the chapter. You may want to use the introduction as a starting point. Be sure to include the following topics:

1. The Natural Life
2. The Spiritual Life
3. No Condemnation
4. Free from the Law
5. A New Mind Set
6. Living According to the Spirit

II. PART TWO
A. BIBLE STUDY APPLICATION

1. Introduction

   The Bible Study Application section contains 10 questions that provide an opportunity to examine what the Bible says about the importance of living in the Spirit, and to discuss how the principles of a Spirit-filled life can be applied to our lives today.

2. Procedure

   Select Small Group Leaders. Ask for volunteers or select four small group leaders. Then assign each small group leader a number from 1-4. (This can be done beforehand to save time.) Ask the small group leaders to write their numbers on large sheets of white paper so that they can be seen from a distance.

   Divide into Small Groups. Inform the participants that they will be separated into four small groups. Each group will study a different set of questions and then will present their findings to the larger group at the end of the study period. The questions should be assigned as follows:

   Group #1: A Better Way (questions 1-5)

   Group #2: Where Do You Live? (questions 6-7)

   Group #3: The Practice of Christian Living (questions 8-9)

   Group #4: The Privileges of Christian Living (question 10)

   Allow Participants to Count Off by Fours. Then ask them to follow the small group leader who is holding their assigned number. Identify the location of each group. (These locations can be pre-printed on a sheet of paper, photocopied, and distributed to save time.) Participants should then assemble into smaller groups in their respective meeting areas.

B. SMALL GROUP STUDY
1. Small Group Leaders
Each group will have one topic to explore. For each topic, there are several questions and related Scripture references to stimulate discussion.

2. Sharing Insights
After 15 minutes, designate someone who will summarize the small group discussion within the larger body of participants. Remind the designated person that she or he will only have two minutes to present.

C. LARGE GROUP PRESENTATIONS
Reconvene the Group. Call the small groups back together.

Explain the Procedure. Explain that a representative of each small group will share that group's reflections on the Bible Study Application questions with the larger group. It may be necessary to pose questions which require them to relate their discussion of Scripture to modern life.

Remind Small Group Representatives of the Time. Remind each group representative that he or she should try to summarize the group's discussion in two minutes.

Allow up to two minutes to discuss each group's presentation.

D. LARGE GROUP STUDY*

Personal Application and Church Ministry Discussion. If time permits, the larger group can then discuss the Personal Application and Church Ministry questions together.

1. Introduction

   The Personal Application section contains five questions which encourage the participants to consider the teaching in light of their own lives. The Church Ministry section contains three questions which address the implications for the congregation as a whole.

2. Sharing Insights

   This discussion should be open-ended and voluntary. The sharing of personal insights or recommendations for church ministry should be encouraged but not required. The group may have quite a bit to say. Watch the clock! Stop them after 10 minutes.

*Answers are not provided for the Personal Application or Church Ministry sections because of the personal or specific nature of the questions.

E. PREPARATION FOR NEXT MEETING

Assignment. Have the participants read Chapter Eight, "Live to Love" and review the questions in preparation for next week's session. Encourage them to come to the next session prepared to share their insights on the content of the chapter.

You may also want to assign small groups or questions to facilitate next week's meeting time.

F. CLOSING PRAYER
Hold hands, form a circle, and ask for specific prayer requests. Then ask for several volunteers to pray, keeping the prayer requests in mind.

ANSWERS TO BIBLE STUDY APPLICATION

A Better Way
The Law was perfect and holy, but humankind is imperfect and carnal. The Israelites struggled in vain to keep the commandments. Thank God, there is a better way! Through Jesus Christ, God has condemned sin and at the same time made it possible for us to escape condemnation.

1. Read Jeremiah 31:31-33 and Hebrews 8:6-10. Use these verses to answer the following questions.
   a) What is different about the new covenant?
      The new covenant is better. God replaces the external law with an internal law.
   b) Where is the Law in the new covenant?
      God puts His laws in the minds of His people and writes them on their hearts.

2. Read Ezekiel 36:26-27. Use these verses to answer the following questions.

   a) What will God give us?

   A new heart and a new spirit.

   b) What will He take away?

   He will take away our heart of stone and give us a heart of flesh.

   c) What else will God give us?

   He will put His Spirit inside of us.

   d) What will His Spirit within us cause us to do?

   God's Spirit will cause us to follow His way and obey His Word.

3. Why do you think that Paul uses the term "the law of the Spirit of life"?

   The Holy Spirit gives life to those who belong to Jesus Christ.

4. Why do you think that Paul uses the term "the law of sin and death"?

   We all have sinned and fallen short of the glory of God, and the wages of sin is death.

5. Why has God made it possible for us to escape condemnation?

   God loves us so much that He sacrificed His Son to provide a way for those who believe in Him to have everlasting life.

Where Do You Live?

As a man thinks in his heart, so is he (Proverbs 23:7). Our mind set (what we think about) affects our actions, our attitudes, and our lifestyle. If we want to live in the Spirit, we must allow the Word of God and the power of the Holy Spirit to change how we think.

6. According to the following verses, on what are we to set our minds?
   a) The Word and the ways of God.
   b) On what the Spirit desires.
   c) On things that are true, honest, just, pure, lovely, of good report, virtuous, and praiseworthy.
   d) On things above (in heaven).

7. Match the following Scripture references with what the Word says concerning the mind set of the believer.
   g. We have been given a sound mind.
   c. We have the mind of Christ.
   h. We are to be sober-minded or self-controlled.
   b. We should love the Lord our God with all our minds.
   d. We should take every thought captive to the knowledge of Christ.
   e. We should be like-minded or one in mind with the Holy Spirit, having the same love, humility, and purpose.
   f. We should not be worried or anxious about anything.
   a. We will have perfect peace as we keep our minds on God and trust in Him.

The Practice of Christian Living

It is humanly impossible to live the Christian life. But the Holy Spirit gives us the power to do it. The Holy Spirit changes us from the inside out. In addition to producing fruit, the Holy Spirit provides power to help us do God's will.

8. Read Galatians 5:16-22. Use these verses to answer the following questions.

   a) What is different about Christians who live by the power of the Holy Spirit?

   They do not gratify the desires of the sinful nature.

   b) Can we follow the sinful nature and the Spirit at the same time?

   No, they are contrary to one another.

   c) What are some of the physical activities or works which are produced in the lives of those who live according to the flesh?

   The works of the flesh are adultery, fornication, uncleanness, lasciviousness, idolatry, witchcraft, hatred, variance, emulations, wrath, strife, seditions, heresies, envyings, murders, drunkenness, revellings, and activities like these.

   d) What are the nine spiritual qualities or the fruit that is produced in the lives of those who live according to the Spirit?

   The fruit of the Spirit is love, joy, peace, longsuffering, gentleness, goodness, faith, meekness, and temperance.

9. Match the following Scripture references to the tasks which the Holy Spirit performs in the life of the believer.

d. He helps us love.

a. He helps us witness for Christ and know what to say.

b. He helps us pray.

c. He teaches us all things.

The Privileges of Christian Living

As we surrender our lives completely to Christ and follow the principles of the Word of God and the leading of the Holy Spirit, we will experience the blessings of God.

10. Read Romans 8:1-27 a second time. What are some of the wonderful blessings that we receive as a result of living according to the Spirit?

a) We are able to escape condemnation.

b) We are set free from the Law.

c) Living in the Spirit fulfills the righteous requirements of the Law.

d) Our mind operates in life and peace.

e) We have the power to put to death the sinful deeds of the flesh so that we will live.

f) We are given the wonderful privilege of being the sons (or children) of God.

g) We do not have a spirit of slavery or fear, but instead we have the spirit of sonship (or adoption into God's family with rights and privileges).

h) We have the inner witness of the Holy Spirit that we are God's children.

i) The Holy Spirit helps us in our weakness; He helps us pray, and He intercedes for us in accordance with God's will.

CHAPTER EIGHT

LIVE TO LOVE

Lesson format for sessions of 90 minutes or more:

PART ONE		PART TWO	
ACTIVITY	TIME	ACTIVITY	TIME
Opening Prayer	5 min.	Small Group Study	20 min.
Scripture Reading	5 min.	Large Group Presentations	20 min.
Scripture Search	5 min.	Large Group Discussion	10 min.
Chapter Highlights	20 min.	Closing Prayer	5 min.

For sessions of less than 90 minutes, use PART ONE only and assign the Bible Study Application section as homework.

LESSON AIMS: At the end of this two-part session, the participant should be able to: a) describe how God has demonstrated His love for us; b) understand the importance of loving God; c) understand the importance of loving others.

I. PART ONE
A. OPENING PRAYER

Open the session with prayer. Include the request that each participant would receive the following:

- An increased awareness of God's love for us.
- A greater understanding of how we can show that we love God.
- A greater desire to love our neighbor as ourselves.

B. SCRIPTURE SEARCH

1. Ask someone to read Mark 12:28-34 aloud to the group.

2. After the Scripture has been read, define the following:

   Heart — the center of our physical and spiritual life.

   Soul — the seat of our emotions (e.g., feelings, desires, appetites, aspirations, and affections).

   Mind — the seat of our understanding, knowledge, and intelligence.

   Strength — our ability or might.

   Neighbor — According to Jesus, any other person of any race or religion with whom we live or whom we chance to meet.

3. Ask for volunteers to give examples to answer the following questions:

   a) How can we love God with all our hearts?

   b) How can we love God with all our souls?

   c) How can we love God with all our minds?

   d) How can we love God with all our strength?

   e) How can we love our neighbor as ourselves?

   Answers will vary.

C. CHAPTER HIGHLIGHTS

Using Chapter Eight as background, give a general overview of the chapter. You may want to use the chapter's introduction as a starting point. Be sure to include the following topics:

1. Showing God's Love
2. Loving the Lord
3. Loving Your Neighbor
4. Immortal Love

II. PART TWO
A. BIBLE STUDY APPLICATION

1. Introduction

   The Bible Study Application section contains 10 questions that provide an opportunity to examine what the Bible says about giving and receiving God's love.

2. Procedure

   Select Small Group Leaders. Ask for volunteers or select four small group leaders. Then assign each small group leader a number from 1-4. (This can be done beforehand to save time.) Ask the small group leaders to write their numbers on large sheets of white paper so that they can be seen from a distance.

   Divide into Small Groups. Inform the participants that they will be separated into four small groups. Each group will study a different set of questions and then will present their findings to the larger group at the end of the study period. The questions should be assigned as follows:

Group #1: Receiving God's Love (questions 1-2)

Group #2: Responding to God's Love (questions 3-4)

Group #3: Demonstrating God's Love, Part 1 (questions 5-7)

Group #4: Demonstrating God's Love, Part 2 (questions 8-10)

Allow Participants to Count Off by Fours. Then ask them to follow the small group leader who is holding their assigned number. Identify the location of each group. (These locations can be pre-printed on a sheet of paper, photocopied, and distributed to save time.) Participants should then assemble into smaller groups in their respective meeting areas.

B. SMALL GROUP STUDY

1. Small Group Leaders

Each group will have one topic to explore. For each topic, there are several questions and related Scripture references to stimulate discussion.

2. Sharing Insights

After 15 minutes, designate someone who will summarize the small group discussion within the larger body of participants. Remind the designated person that she or he will only have two minutes to present.

C. LARGE GROUP PRESENTATIONS

Reconvene the Group. Call the small groups back together.

Explain the Procedure. Explain that a representative of each small group will share that group's reflections on the Bible Study Application questions with the larger group. It may be necessary to pose questions which require them to relate their discussion of Scripture to modern life.

Remind Small Group Representatives of the Time. Remind each group representative that he or she should try to summarize the group's discussion in two minutes. Allow up to two minutes to discuss each group's presentation.

D. LARGE GROUP STUDY*
Personal Application and Church Ministry Discussion. If time permits, the larger group can then discuss the Personal Application and Church Ministry questions together.

1. Introduction

   The Personal Application section contains five questions which encourage the participants to consider the teaching in light of their own lives. The Church Ministry section contains three questions which address some implications for the congregation as a whole.

2. Sharing Insights

   This discussion should be open-ended and voluntary. The sharing of personal insights or recommendations for church ministry should be encouraged but not required. The group may have quite a bit to say. Watch the clock! Stop them after 10 minutes.

*Answers are not provided for the Personal Application and Church Ministry sections because of the personal or specific nature of the questions.

E. PREPARATION FOR NEXT MEETING
Assignment. Have the participants read Chapter Eight, "Count the Cost" and review the questions in preparation for next week's session. Encourage them to come to the next session prepared to share their insights on the content of the chapter.

You may also want to assign small groups or questions to facilitate next week's meeting time.

F. CLOSING PRAYER
Hold hands, form a circle, and ask for specific prayer requests. Then ask for several volunteers to pray, keeping the prayer requests in mind.

ANSWERS TO BIBLE STUDY APPLICATION

Receiving God's Love
Love is the greatest gift of all (1 Corinthians 13:13). Godly love or *agape* is an unselfish seeking of another's good without regard to their worthiness. God has made His gift of love available to all who will receive it.

1. Read John 3:16-17; Romans 5:8; and 1 John 4:9-10. Use these verses to answer the following questions.
   a) Who did God love?

God loved all of the people of the world, in spite of our sins.

b) What did He do because of His love?

He gave His Son Jesus to die for us.

c) When we receive God's gift of love, what do we get?

Eternal life; we are saved from the penalty of sin which is death.

2. Match the following Scripture references with the way that God's love was manifested in Jesus Christ.

a. Coming to seek and save the lost.

b. Praying for His enemies.

d. Sending the Holy Spirit.

c. Dying for us.

f. Interceding for us.

g. Washing away our sins.

e. Giving Himself for us.

Responding to God's Love

Knowing that God's love is unconditional frees us from trying to be perfect or trying to earn His love by our performance. Knowing that God's love is continual also frees us from the fear of losing it. But this same knowledge creates in us a desire to please Him and to show Him that we love Him in return.

3. How can we show that we love God?

a) We can show that we love God by obeying His Word.

b) We can show that we love God by obeying His Word and abiding in Him.

c) We can show that we love God by loving His children and obeying His Word.

4. Read 1 John 4:7-21. Use these verses to answer the following questions.

a) Where does love come from?

Love comes from God.

b) How has God revealed His love to us?

He sent His only Son to be the atoning sacrifice for our sins so that we might have eternal life through Him.

c) If we love God, what will we do?

If we love God, we will love one another.

d) If we love one another, what does it show?

It shows that God abides in us because He has given us His Holy Spirit.

e) Why has this love been given to us?

We have been given God's love so that we can have confidence on the Day of Judgment, with assurance and boldness to face Him, because as He is, so are we in this world.

f) What does love free us from?

We are free from fear because our punishment has been borne by Jesus Christ and we have been made perfect (righteous) by His love.

g) Why do we love?

We love because God first loved us.

h) How can we tell whether our love is true?

We don't go by what we say (or what we think we

feel); we look at the evidence. If we don't love others, then we don't truly love God.

Demonstrating God's Love to Others

The highest expression of our spirituality is seen when we demonstrate the love of God. The love of God is not a feeling. It is not shown by an emotional or verbal commitment. God's love is demonstrated by action. "Let us not love in word or speech but in deed and in truth" (1 John 3:18, RSV).

5. Read John 13:34-35. Use these verses to answer the following questions.
   a) Whose example should we follow?
   We should follow Jesus' example.
   b) How would you describe the way He loved?
   Jesus' love for us was divine *(agape)*, unchanging, everlasting, and self-sacrificing.
   c) What is the result when we practice this kind of love?
   People will know that we are Christians.

6. Read 1 Corinthians 13:4-7. Use the following verses to determine how Christians should demonstrate God's love to others.
   a) Love is demonstrated by patience and kindness toward others.
   b) Love is demonstrated by being polite and forgiving.
   c) Love is demonstrated by rejoicing in the truth.
   d) Love is demonstrated by providing protection, extending trust, offering hope, and supporting others through trial or difficulty.

7. How are we able to love others with God's love?

   The love of God is poured out into our hearts by the Holy Spirit. The Holy Spirit continues to flood our hearts with love so that we can experience the love of God and have God's love for other believers.

8. Read Luke 6:27-36. Use these verses to answer the following questions.

   a) What should we do to our enemies?

      We should love our enemies.

   b) What should we do to those who curse us?

      We should pray for (bless) those who curse us.

   c) What should we do to those who challenge us?

      We should be gracious to them.

   d) What should we do to those who would defraud us?

      We should have mercy on them and give to them.

   e) What should we do to those who beg from us?

      We should give to them.

   f) What should we do to those who would steal from us?

      We should let them keep that which they have stolen.

   g) If we do these things and expect nothing in return, what will we receive?

      We will receive a heavenly reward.

   h) If we do these things, whose example are we following?

      We are following God's example and are showing that we are His children.

9. Read Romans 12:9-21. Match each verse with the characteristic of love that it describes. (Some verses may describe more than one characteristic.)

   c. fervent

   g. sympathetic

   i. doing right

   k. forgiving

   a. sincere

   h. humble

   b. devoted

   l. helpful

   j. peaceful

   d. joyful in hope

   m. good

   e. generous

   f. kind

   b. respectful

   d. patient in affliction

   g. compassionate

   e. hospitable

   d. faithful in prayer

10. God hates sin but loves the sinner. Use the following verses to identify what we should hate.

   a) We should love righteousness and hate wickedness.

   b) We should love good and hate evil.

   c) We should not love the world or the things in the world.

CHAPTER NINE

FORGIVING AND FORGIVEN

Lesson format for sessions of 90 minutes or more:

PART ONE		PART TWO	
ACTIVITY	TIME	ACTIVITY	TIME
Opening Prayer	5 min.	Small Group Study	20 min.
Scripture Reading	5 min.	Large Group Presentations	20 min.
Scripture Search	5 min.	Large Group Discussion	10 min.
Chapter Highlights	20 min.	Closing Prayer	5 min.

For sessions of less than 90 minutes, use PART ONE only and assign the Bible Study Application section as homework.

LESSON AIMS: At the end of this two-part session, the participant should be able to: a) describe how God has provided forgiveness for our sins; b) understand the importance of forgiving ourselves; c) understand the importance of forgiving others.

I. PART ONE
A. OPENING PRAYER

Open the session with prayer. Include the request that each participant would receive the following:

- A greater understanding of our need to receive God's forgiveness.
- A clearer understanding of the importance of forgiving ourselves.
- An increased awareness of the importance of forgiving others.

B. SCRIPTURE SEARCH

1. Ask someone to read 1 John 2:1-6 aloud to the group.
2. Ask for volunteers to answer the following questions:

    a) To whom was this passage written?

      This passage was written to believers in Jesus Christ.

    b) What work is Jesus currently doing for us in heaven?

      When we sin, Jesus speaks to the Father in our defense.

    c) What work did Jesus complete for us on earth?

      Jesus was the atoning sacrifice for our sins.

    d) What does it mean "to know Him"?

      To know Him means to believe in Him and to belong to Him.

    e) If we know Him, what should we do?

      As Christians who believe in and belong to Jesus Christ, we must obey His commands and walk in the Spirit.

C. CHAPTER HIGHLIGHTS

Before the discussing the chapter, explain the meaning of **Jesus as our atoning sacrifice.**

• Read Romans 3:22-26 aloud.

• Explain that the word **atone** involves three parts:
  – to satisfy the law and the justice of God;
  – to effect reconciliation between God and humankind (to change from enmity to love);
  – to deliver by a ransom or payment of a price.

Using Chapter Nine as background, give a general overview of the chapter. You may want to use the chapter's introduction as a starting point. Be sure to include the following topics:

1. Our Sin
2. God's Love and Forgiveness
3. God's Forgiven People
4. Our Assurance of Forgiveness

II. PART TWO
A. BIBLE STUDY APPLICATION

1. Introduction

   The Bible Study Application section contains 10 questions that provide an opportunity to examine what the Bible says about giving and receiving forgiveness.

2. Procedure

   Select Small Group Leaders. Ask for volunteers or select four small group leaders. Then assign each small group leader a number from 1-4. (This can be done beforehand to save time.) Ask the small group leaders to write their numbers on large sheets of white paper so that they can be seen from a distance.

Divide into Small Groups. Inform the participants that they will be separated into four small groups. Each group will study a different set of questions and then will present their findings to the larger group at the end of the study period. The questions should be assigned as follows:

Group #1: Receiving Forgiveness (questions 1-4)

Group #2: The Power of the Blood (questions 5-6)

Group #3: The Promise of Redemption (questions 7-8)

Group #4: Forgiving Others (questions 9-10)

Allow Participants to Count Off by Fours. Then ask them to follow the small group leader who is holding their assigned number. Identify the location of each group. (These locations can be pre-printed on a sheet of paper, photocopied, and distributed to save time.) Participants should then assemble into smaller groups in their respective meeting areas.

B. SMALL GROUP STUDY

1. Small Group Leaders

   Each group will have one topic to explore. For each topic, there are several questions and related Scripture references to stimulate discussion.

2. Sharing Insights

After 15 minutes, designate someone who will summarize the small group discussion within the larger body of participants. Remind the designated person that she or he will only have two minutes to present.

C. LARGE GROUP PRESENTATIONS

Reconvene the Group. Call the small groups back together.

Explain the Procedure. Explain that a representative of each small group will share that group's reflections on the Bible Study Application questions with the larger group. It may be necessary to pose questions which require them to relate their discussion of Scripture to modern life.

Remind Small Group Representatives of the Time. Remind each group representative that he or she should try to summarize the group's discussion in two minutes. Allow up to two minutes to discuss each group's presentation.

D. LARGE GROUP STUDY*

Personal Application and Church Ministry Discussion. If time permits, the larger group can then discuss the Personal Application and Church Ministry questions together.

1. Introduction
   The Personal Application section contains five questions which encourage participants to consider the teaching in light of their own lives. The Church

Ministry section contains three questions which address some implications for the congregation as a whole.

2. Sharing Insights
   This discussion should be open-ended and voluntary. The sharing of personal insights or recommendations for church ministry should be encouraged but not required. The group may have quite a bit to say. Watch the clock! Stop them after 10 minutes.

*Answers are not provided for the Personal Application and Church Ministry sections because of the personal or specific nature of the questions.

E. PREPARATION FOR NEXT MEETING
   Assignment. Have the participants read Chapter Ten, "Count the Cost" and review the questions in preparation for next week's session. Encourage them to come to the next session prepared to share their insights on the content of the chapter.

   You may also want to assign small groups or questions to facilitate next week's meeting time.

F. CLOSING PRAYER
   Hold hands, form a circle, and ask for specific prayer requests. Then ask for several volunteers to pray, keeping the prayer requests in mind.

ANSWERS TO BIBLE STUDY APPLICATION

Receiving God's Forgiveness

God offers us forgiveness through Jesus Christ because He loves us. "This is love: not that we loved God, but that he loved us and sent his Son as an atoning sacrifice for our sins" (1 John 4:10, NIV).

1. Match the following verses with the characteristic of God's forgiveness that it describes.
   c. available
   a. compassionate
   b. complete

2. Why did Jesus come?
   Jesus came destroy the devil's work and to reconcile us to God. Jesus rose to empower us to live the lives to which we have been called.

3. We can learn much from Jesus' ministry on earth. Use the verses from the Book of Luke and the related Scriptures to answer the following questions.
   a) What role does repentance play in receiving forgiveness?
   Repentance is the attitude that results when the sinner recognizes his or her own condition and turns to God to ask for forgiveness.
   b) What role does confession play in receiving forgiveness?
   Confession of sin is followed by pardon.
   c) What role does faith play in receiving forgiveness?

113

Forgiveness is a gift from God that we receive by believing in Christ's work and God's Word.

d) What should be our response when we are forgiven?

We should love God.

4. After we have received forgiveness through Jesus Christ, how can we keep our lives free from sin?
   a) Through prayer
   b) Through reading and obeying God's Word
   c) By walking in love
   d) By hoping in Christ

Forgiven

There are many religious terms which are used to describe the forgiveness we have received from God through Jesus Christ. Let's make sure we know what the Bible says about what we speak and sing about.

5. We often sing about the blood, but do we really know why? Read Leviticus 17:11 and Hebrews 9:22. Use these verses to answer the following questions.
   a) What is the significance of the blood?

      The life of the flesh is in the blood.

   b) What did the Law require?

      The Law required the shedding of blood; without the shedding of blood there is no remission of sins.

6. Use the following verses to discuss the importance of the blood of Jesus.
   a) According to the prophesy in Matthew 1:21, who

would save us from our sin?

It was prophesied that Jesus would save people from their sins.

b) What did Jesus announce in Matthew 26:28?

Jesus announced that the shedding of His blood created a new covenant which provides the remission of sins.

c) What did Jesus obtain for us?

In Jesus, we have redemption or the forgiveness of sins, and we have been rescued from the dominion (power) of darkness to become the children of God.

d) What did Jesus give in exchange?

By His own blood, Jesus obtained eternal redemption for us.

e) Why is the blood important?

The blood of Jesus cleanses us from all sin.

f) Why did Jesus do this for us?

Because of His love for us, Jesus washed us from our sins in His own blood.

7. We often talk about being redeemed, but do we know what it means? Use the following verses to discuss the relationship between redemption and forgiveness.

a) What does redemption mean? If we are redeemed, what should we do?

Redemption means that we now belong to God. Therefore, we should glorify Him.

b) Who was sent to redeem us?

God sent Jesus to redeem us from the Law so that we might become the children of God.

c) How did we receive redemption?

We were redeemed through the shedding of Christ's precious blood for us. In Him, we have received forgiveness for sin and been given the grace of God.

8. The Bible talks about a new covenant. Read Matthew 26:26-28; Hebrews 8:6; 13:20. Use these verses to answer the following questions.

a) How has our new covenant with God been established?

Our new covenant has been established in Christ's blood.

b) How does the new covenant compare to the old?

The new covenant is better and it is established on better promises.

c) How long will the new covenant last?

The new covenant is an everlasting covenant.

Forgiving Others

We are a fellowship of sinners saved by the grace of God. As we allow the Holy Spirit to work in and through our lives, He will enable us to forgive others just as we have received forgiveness through Christ.

9. According to the following verses, why should we forgive?

a) We are to ask God to forgive us as we forgive others. Therefore if we forgive, we will be forgiven.

b) We are to forgive others because Christ has forgiven us.

10. Read Matthew 18:23-35 and Galatians 6:7. Use these verses to answer the following questions.

a) Should there be a limit to our forgiveness?

Jesus' answer of 490 ("seventy times seven") implies that we should forgive freely.

b) What kind of consequences are given for unforgiveness in this parable or illustration?

The consequences for unforgiveness are severe.

c) Describe the relationship between giving and receiving forgiveness.

We are forgiven as we forgive.

CHAPTER TEN

COUNT THE COST

Lesson format for sessions of 90 minutes or more:

PART ONE		PART TWO	
ACTIVITY	TIME	ACTIVITY	TIME
Opening Prayer	5 min.	Small Group Study	20 min.
Scripture Reading	5 min.	Large Group Presentations	20 min.
Scripture Search	5 min.	Large Group Discussion	10 min.
Chapter Highlights	20 min.	Closing Prayer	5 min.

For sessions of less than 90 minutes, use PART ONE only and assign the Bible Study Application section as homework.

LESSON AIMS: At the end of this two-part session, the participant should be able to: a) understand the cost of spirituality; b) identify the type of sacrifice and commitment that discipleship requires; c) understand the benefits and the blessing that we receive from God in return.

119

I. PART ONE
A. OPENING PRAYER

Open the session with prayer. Include the request that each participant would receive the following:

- An understanding that the benefits and blessings of following Jesus far outweigh the cost.
- A greater commitment to follow Christ.

B. SCRIPTURE SEARCH

1. Ask someone to read Mark 8:34-38 aloud to the group.
2. Ask for volunteers to answer the following questions:

    a) To whom was Jesus speaking?

    Jesus was speaking to anyone who wants to be His follower. In other words, He is speaking to us.

    b) Jesus contrasts the pursuit of worldly things to the pursuit of spiritual things. Which does He consider most valuable?

    Jesus considers salvation of our soul to be more valuable than gaining all that the world has to offer.

    c) What do you think it means to be ashamed of Jesus?

    Answers will vary.

    d) What event is Jesus speaking of when He says "When he comes in his Father's glory with the holy angels"?

    He is speaking of His second coming; see also John 14:2-3.

    e) Why would we not want Him to be ashamed of us at this important time?

Because we want to be with Him; see also

Colossians 3:4 and 2 Timothy 4:8.

C. CHAPTER HIGHLIGHTS

Before the discussing the chapter, clarify the following:

- Explain that a disciple is a learner or a follower who adheres to the doctrines or principles of another.
- Use this definition to discuss whether or not we should consider ourselves to be disciples of Jesus today.
- If possible, have each person briefly state his or her personal opinion of discipleship. (Be sure to maintain an atmosphere in which differences are treated respectfully.)

Using Chapter Ten as background, give a general overview of the chapter. You may want to use the chapter's introduction as a starting point. Be sure to include the following topics:

1. Spiritual Sacrifice
2. Taking Up the Cross
3. Denying Yourself
4. Following Jesus
5. Finding Life
6. Not Ashamed

II. PART TWO
A. BIBLE STUDY APPLICATION

1. Introduction

The Bible Study Application section contains eight questions that provide an opportunity to examine what the Bible says about the costs and benefits of following Jesus.

2. Procedure

Select Small Group Leaders. Ask for volunteers or select four small group leaders. Then assign each small group leader a number from 1-4. (This can be done beforehand to save time.) Ask the small group leaders to write their numbers on large sheets of white paper so that they can be seen from a distance.

Divide into Small Groups. Inform the participants that they will be separated into four small groups. Each group will study a different set of questions and then will present their findings to the larger group at the end of the study period. The questions should be assigned as follows:

Group #1: How Discipleship Affects Our Mind and Body (questions 1 and 2)

Group #2: How Discipleship Affects Our Goals and Service (questions 3 and 4)

Group #3: How Discipleship Affects Our Will and Attitudes (questions 5 and 6)

Group #4: How Discipleship Affects Our Relationships and Conversation (questions 7 and 8)

Allow Participants to Count Off by Fours. Then ask them to follow the small group leader who is holding their assigned number. Identify the location of each group. (These locations can be pre-printed on a sheet of paper, photocopied, and distributed to save time.) Participants should then assemble into smaller groups in their respective meeting areas.

B. SMALL GROUP STUDY
1. Small Group Leaders
Each group will have one topic to explore. For each topic, there are several questions and related Scripture references to stimulate discussion.

2. Sharing Insights
After 15 minutes, designate someone who will summarize the small group discussion within the larger body of participants. Remind the designated person that she or he will only have two minutes to present.

C. LARGE GROUP PRESENTATIONS
Reconvene the Group. Call the small groups back together.

Explain the Procedure. Explain that a representative of each small group will share that group's reflections on the Bible Study Application questions with the larger group. It may be necessary to pose questions which require them to relate their discussion of Scripture to modern life.

Remind Small Group Representatives of the Time. Remind each group representative that he or she should try to summarize the group's discussion in two minutes. Allow up to two minutes to discuss each group's presentation.

D. LARGE GROUP STUDY*

Personal Application and Church Ministry Discussion. If time permits, the larger group can then discuss the Personal Application and Church Ministry questions together.

1. Introduction

   The Personal Application section contains five questions which encourage participants to consider the teaching in light of their own lives. The Church Ministry section contains three questions which address some implications for the congregation as a whole.

2. Sharing Insights

   This discussion should be open-ended and voluntary. The sharing of personal insights or recommendations for church ministry should be encouraged but not required. The group may have quite a bit to say. Watch the clock! Stop them after 10 minutes.

*Answers are not provided for the Personal Application and Church Ministry sections because of the personal or specific nature of the questions.

E. PREPARATION FOR NEXT MEETING

Assignment. Have the participants read Chapter Eleven, "Open for Business" and review the questions in preparation for next week's session. Encourage them to come to the next session prepared to share their insights on the content of the chapter.

You may also want to assign small groups or questions to facilitate next week's meeting time.

F. CLOSING PRAYER

Hold hands, form a circle, and ask for specific prayer requests. Then ask for several volunteers to pray, keeping the prayer requests in mind.

ANSWERS TO BIBLE STUDY APPLICATION

Becoming Christ's Disciple
Next to His redemptive work on the Cross, Jesus' most important ministry on earth was calling a group of willing and dedicated disciples who would impact the world.

Jesus ministered to the crowds because of His love and compassion. But God cannot use people who will follow Him only for the benefits. The Word of God says, "Jesus Christ is the same yesterday and today and forever" (Hebrews 13:8, NRSV). Jesus is calling committed followers who have counted the cost and upon whom He can depend.

1. Use the following verses to identify how discipleship affects our **minds.**
   Count the cost:
   a) We are to love the Lord with all of our minds.
   b) We are to renew (transform) our minds with the Word of God.
   c) We are to cast down any thoughts or imaginations that do not agree with the Word and the will of God and bring every thought into the obedience of Christ.
   Identify the benefits:

d) We have the mind of Christ.

e) God gives us a sound mind.

f) God writes His laws in our minds and we become His people.

2. Use the following verses to identify how discipleship affects our **bodies.**

Count the cost:

a) We are to present our bodies as a living sacrifice to God.

b) We are to glorify God in our bodies.

c) We are to keep our bodies under control or subjection.

Consider Jesus' example:

d) He gave His body and blood to create a new covenant for us.

e) He bore our sins in His body so that we might receive righteousness. He was wounded that we might be healed.

Identify the benefits:

f) We are free from serving sin.

g) We will live.

h) We will receive a glorified body.

3. Use the following verses to identify how discipleship affects our **goals** and **pursuits.**

Count the cost:

a) We are to store up treasure in heaven, not on earth.

b) We cannot serve both God and money.

c) We are to put God first and seek the things of God before all else.

d) We are to set our affection on things above (in heaven) and count our life as hidden with Christ in God.

e) We are to turn away from evil and to seek peace and pursue it.

f) We cannot love the world because we love the Father.

Consider Jesus' example:

g) Jesus did not please Himself, instead He sought to please God.

Identify the benefits:

h) When we seek the Lord and pursue righteousness, God will give it to us.

i) God is a rewarder of those who diligently seek Him.

j) God promises that He will never leave us or forsake us.

4. Use the following verses to identify how discipleship affects our **service.**

Count the cost:

a) We are to do the will of God from the hearts.

b) In whatever we do, we should work heartily as unto the Lord, doing everything in the name of Jesus Christ and give thanks to God.

c) If we will serve Jesus, we must also follow Him.

Consider Jesus' example:

d) Jesus worked diligently and redeemed the time.

e) Jesus took the form of a servant and humbled Himself to die on the Cross for our salvation and for God's glory.

127

Identify the benefits:

f) If we serve Jesus, we will receive honor from the Lord.

g) God will repay each one according to his works.

h) God will remember your service.

i) As we obey and serve God, we will be blessed in our deeds.

5. Use the following verses to identify how discipleship affects our **will.**

Count the cost:

a) We are to trust in the Lord with all our hearts and not rely on our own insight, understanding, or judgment apart from His Word. We are to acknowledge Him in all our ways—our attitudes and actions should show that we belong to Him.

b) We are to obey God's commands.

Consider Jesus' example:

c) Even when facing the cross, Jesus laid aside His own desire and asked that the Father's will be done.

d) Jesus taught us to pray that the Father's will would be done on earth as it is done in heaven.

e) Jesus came to do the will of the Father.

Identify the benefits:

f) We will enter into the kingdom of heaven.

g) We will become members of the family of God.

h) We shall be loved by Jesus and by God the Father.

6. Use the following verses to identify how discipleship affects our **attitudes.**

   Count the cost:

   a) Through Christ, we can learn to be content despite the circumstances.

   b) We are to put off anger, wrath, malice, blasphemy, filthy communication, and lying.

   c) We are to put on (clothe ourselves in) tender mercies, kindness, humility, meekness, long-suffering, forgiveness, love, peace, the wisdom of the Word, and thanksgiving.

   Consider Jesus' example:

   d) Jesus was meek and lowly of heart.

   e) Jesus was compassionate.

   f) Jesus was humble.

   Identify the benefits:

   g) We shall receive blessing (true happiness) and great reward in heaven, as well as benefits and inheritance on earth.

   h) We will produce the fruit of the Spirit.

   i) Godliness with contentment is great gain.

   j) When God looks at our hearts, He will treasure what He finds.

7. Use the following verses to identify how discipleship affects our **relationships**.

   Count the cost:

   a) We are to love Jesus more than our earthly relationships.

   Consider Jesus' example:

   b) Jesus put doing God's will before His family relationships.

Identify the benefits:

c) We shall receive a one hundred-fold return for what we have sacrificed and shall have everlasting life.

8. Use the following verses to identify how discipleship affects our **conversation.**

Count the cost:

a) We will give an account to God for every idle word we speak.

b) Our conversation identifies what is in our hearts.

c) We are not to speak from ourselves but to agree with God and give Him glory.

d) We are to speak the truth in love.

e) We are to speak the Word of God with boldness.

f) We are to repay insult with blessing and keep our tongue from evil and deceitful speech.

g) We should always be prepared to give an answer about our hope in Christ and do so with gentleness and respect.

h) We must control our tongue.

Consider Jesus' example:

i) Jesus spoke words of life-giving force.

j) Jesus spoke as directed by the Father.

Identify the benefits:

k) If we love to speak words of life, we will eat of the fruit of life.

l) We will love life and see good days.

CHAPTER ELEVEN

OPEN FOR BUSINESS

Lesson format for sessions of 90 minutes or more:

PART ONE		PART TWO	
ACTIVITY	TIME	ACTIVITY	TIME
Opening Prayer	5 min.	Small Group Study	20 min.
Scripture Reading	5 min.	Large Group Presentations	20 min.
Scripture Search	5 min.	Large Group Discussion	10 min.
Chapter Highlights	20 min.	Closing Prayer	5 min.

For sessions of less than 90 minutes, use PART ONE only and assign the Bible Study Application section as homework.

LESSON AIMS: At the end of this two-part session, the participant should be able to: a) understand the importance of spiritual work; b) describe how we prepare for spiritual work; c) identify how we are empowered for spiritual work.

I. PART ONE
A. OPENING PRAYER

Open the session with prayer. Include the request that each participant would receive the following:

- An increased understanding of the importance of our jobs as Christians.
- A greater commitment to work for Christ.

B. SCRIPTURE SEARCH

1. Ask someone to read Acts 3:1-10 aloud to the group.
2. Read the following paragraphs, and ask for volunteers to answer the questions:

Peter and John, who represent the church in Jerusalem, were practicing their spirituality. The lame man at the gate of the temple represents the world—humanity at large, with all its needs—at the doorstep of the Church. As His disciples, Peter and John were carrying on the ministry of Jesus Christ.

a) Describe the time that this story takes place in terms of the life of Jesus Christ.

Jesus had been crucified, resurrected, and ascended to heaven.

b) Describe the time that this story takes place in terms of key events in Church history.

The Holy Spirit had been given, and the Church had received power to be God's witnesses on earth.

c) Describe the time that this story takes place in terms of the life of Peter.

After denying Jesus, Peter was charged to feed the sheep by the resurrected Lord. On the Day of Pentecost, Peter preached to a large crowd with boldness and many were saved.

These were exciting times. This was the beginning of the work to fulfill the Great Commission. God was opening doors, and the disciples were proclaiming the Gospel at every opportunity in spite of rejection and persecution.

d) Were Peter and John too busy to pray?

No

e) Do you think they learned this from Jesus?

Yes

f) What conclusions can we draw from their example?

Answers will vary.

This day was no different from any other. A man who was paralyzed from birth was taken to his usual place outside the temple to beg for money. We are not told who brought him, or his name, but we know that he was there. On this particular day, Peter and John noticed him as he begged for money, and Peter took the time to help him.

g) What conclusions can we draw from Peter's example?

Answers will vary.

h) Do you think he learned about this from Jesus?

Yes

To pray or minister "in the name of Jesus" means to ask or act on His authority so that God alone gets the glory.

i) What happened when Peter ministered in the name of Jesus?

The man received strength in his legs. He leaped up and not only walked—he ran into the temple.

j) Who did the man praise?

He praised God.

C. CHAPTER HIGHLIGHTS

Using Chapter Eleven as background, give a general overview of the chapter. You may want to use the introduction as a starting point. Be sure to include the following topics:

1. The Importance of Spiritual Work
2. The Power of Prayer
3. What Do We Have to Offer?
4. Demonstrating Our Spirituality
5. Spiritual Enterprise

II. PART TWO
A. BIBLE STUDY APPLICATION

1. Introduction

   The Bible Study Application section contains 10 questions that provide an opportunity to examine what the Bible says about the nature and importance of spiritual work.

2. Procedure

   Select Small Group Leaders. Ask for volunteers or select five small group leaders. Then assign each small group leader a number from 1-5. (This can be done beforehand to save time.) Ask the small group leaders to write their numbers on large sheets of white paper so that they can be seen from a distance.

   Divide into Small Groups. Inform the participants that they will be separated into five small groups.

Each group will study a different set of questions and then will present their findings to the larger group at the end of the study period. The questions should be assigned as follows:

Group #1: The Work of Jesus Christ (questions 1 and 2)

Group #2: Prepared for Business (questions 3 and 4)

Group #3: The Nature of Our Business (questions 5 and 6)

Group #4: The Rewards of Our Labor (questions 7 and 8)

Group #5: Quality Control (questions 9 and 10)

Allow Participants to Count Off by Fives. Then ask them to follow the small group leader who is holding their assigned number. Identify the location of each group. (These locations can also be pre-printed on a sheet of paper, photocopied, and distributed to save time.) Participants should then assemble into smaller groups in their respective meeting areas.

B. SMALL GROUP STUDY

1. Small Group Leaders

Each group will have one topic to explore. For each topic, there are several questions and related Scripture references to stimulate discussion.

2. Sharing Insights

After 15 minutes, designate someone who will summarize the small group discussion within the larger body of participants. Remind the designated person that she or he will only have two minutes to present.

C. LARGE GROUP PRESENTATIONS

Reconvene the Group. Call the small groups back together.

Explain the Procedure. Explain that a representative of each small group will share that group's reflections on the Bible Study Application questions with the larger group. It may be necessary to pose questions which require them to relate their discussion of Scripture to modern life.

Remind Small Group Representatives of the Time. Remind each group representative that he or she should try to summarize the group's discussion in two minutes. Allow up to two minutes to discuss each group's presentation.

D. LARGE GROUP STUDY*

Personal Application and Church Ministry Discussion. If time permits, the larger group can then discuss the Personal Application and Church Ministry questions together.

1. Introduction

   The Personal Application section contains five question which encourage the participants to consider the teaching in light of their own lives. The Church Ministry section contains three questions which address some implications for the congregation as a whole.

2. Sharing Insights

   This discussion should be open-ended and voluntary.

The sharing of personal insights or recommendations for church ministry should be encouraged but not required. The group may have quite a bit to say. Watch the clock! Stop them after 10 minutes.

*Answers are not provided for the Personal Application and Church Ministry sections because of the personal or specific nature of the questions.

E. PREPARATION FOR NEXT MEETING
Assignment. Have the participants read Chapter Twelve, "Spiritual Renewal" and review the questions in preparation for next week's session. Encourage them to come to the next session prepared to share their insights on the content of the chapter.

You may also want to assign small groups or questions to facilitate next week's meeting time.

F. CLOSING PRAYER
Hold hands, form a circle, and ask for specific prayer requests. Then ask for several volunteers to pray, keeping the prayer requests in mind.

ANSWERS TO BIBLE STUDY APPLICATION

The Work of Jesus Christ
1. Use the following verses to examine the ministry of Jesus Christ.
   a) What work did Jesus come to finish?
   Jesus came to finish God's work.

b) Describe the relationship between the works of Jesus and the identity of Jesus Christ.

The works were the evidence that Jesus was the Son of God.

c) What kind of works did Jesus do while on earth?

He went about teaching, preaching the Gospel of the kingdom of God, doing good, healing the sick, and delivering those who were oppressed by the devil.

d) Although Jesus was God's Son, He was also human. Who empowered Jesus to do the work?

The Holy Spirit empowered Jesus.

2. Use the following verses to describe how we should relate Jesus' example to our own spiritual work.

a) Describe the relationship between our works and our identity as the children of God.

How we act reveals who we are. By keeping God's commandments and doing works of righteousness, we demonstrate that we are the children of God.

b) What kind of work will we do and why?

Jesus said that we could do even greater works because the Holy Spirit abides with us.

c) What is the first step we must take if we are to do the work of God?

We must believe the Gospel of Jesus Christ.

d) Who empowers us to perform our spiritual work?

The Holy Spirit empowers us.

Prepared for Business

3. Use the following verses to identify how we can become prepared for spiritual business.

   a) By keeping God's Word continually in our hearts and minds, and by making it the guide for our actions.

   b) By maintaining the habit of prayer to draw strength and wisdom from intimate communication with God.

   c) As we obey His commands, we abide in God's love, God reveals Himself to us, and He answers our prayers.

   d) By resisting sin and yielding to the direction of the Holy Spirit.

4. Use the following verses to identify how the Holy Spirit prepares us for spiritual business.

   a) He invites us to receive eternal life.

   b) He counsels us and abides with us.

   c) He teaches us and reminds us of the things of God.

   d) He guides us and reveals truth to us.

   e) He helps us in our weakness and intercedes for us in accordance with God's will.

The Nature of Our Business

5. Match the following verses with the terms that describe how spirituality affects our human relationships.

   b. We should love our enemies.

   a. We should forgive our debtors and enemies.

   g. We should serve others.

　　c. We should love our neighbors as ourselves.

　　e. We should consider others better than ourselves.

　　d. We should love other believers.

　　f. We should show respect to every person regardless of status.

6. Match the following verses with the terms that describe the attitude that we should possess as we work.

　　a. Steadfast and productive

　　e. Thankful

　　c. Zealous

　　d. Generous

　　b. Whole-hearted

　　f. Done in meekness

　　g. Careful

　　h. Ready

The Rewards of Our Labor

7. Use the following verses to identify the purpose of spiritual work.

　　a) Soul-winning

　　b) Serving God

　　c) Pleasing God

　　d) Glorifying God

　　e) Doing the will of God

　　f) Revealing the power of God

8. Use the following verses to identify the rewards that the Lord will provide for His workers.

a) Honor
b) Repayment
c) Good things
d) Remembrance
e) Blessing
f) Eternal life

Quality Control
9. Read 1 Corinthians 3:10-15. Use these verses to answer the following questions.
   a) Who is our foundation?
      Jesus Christ is our foundation.
   b) What will be tested?
      The quality of each man's work will be tested.
   c) Who will be rewarded?
      Those people whose work survives God's testing will be rewarded.
   d) Who will suffer loss?
      Those people whose work does not pass the test will suffer loss. The Scripture implies that this loss is painful.

10. Believers will not be judged for sin; Christ received this judgment. According to the following verses, for what will we be judged or give an account?
    a) The deeds done while in the body.
    b) Every word we speak.

CHAPTER TWELVE

SPIRITUAL RENEWAL

Lesson format for sessions of 90 minutes or more:

PART ONE		PART TWO	
ACTIVITY	TIME	ACTIVITY	TIME
Opening Prayer	5 min.	Small Group Study	20 min.
Scripture Reading	5 min.	Large Group Presentations	20 min.
Scripture Search	5 min.	Large Group Discussion	10 min.
Chapter Highlights	20 min.	Closing Prayer	5 min.

For sessions of less than 90 minutes, use PART ONE only and assign the Bible Study Application section as homework.

LESSON AIMS: At the end of this two-part session, the participant should be able to: a) describe God's agenda for spiritual renewal; b) understand how we become spiritually renewed; c) describe our role in the process of spiritual renewal.

I. PART ONE
A. OPENING PRAYER

Open the session with prayer. Include the request that each participant would receive the following:

• An increased understanding of the meaning of spiritual renewal.

• A greater commitment to submit ourselves to God daily, so that the work of God might continue in us.

B. SCRIPTURE SEARCH

1. Ask someone to read Revelation 21:1-5 aloud to the group.

2. Ask for volunteers to answer the following questions:

   a) How does this passage of Scripture describe the ultimate goal and expectation of our faith in Jesus Christ?

   We will see the outworking and completion of our redemption. Not only will our transformation be completed, God will make all things new. The new earth will become God's headquarters and we will dwell with Him forever.

   b) Unhappiness, pain, sorrow, and death are the effects of sin. In God's presence, what will happen?

   These things will be gone forever. God will wipe away every tear and there will be no more death or mourning or crying or pain. The old order of things will pass away.

   c) Verse 5 says, "He who was seated on the throne said, 'I am making everything new!'" Why do you think that God tells John to write these words?

   Answers will vary.

d) Do you believe that passage is to be taken literally or figuratively?

Answers will vary.

C. CHAPTER HIGHLIGHTS

Using Chapter Twelve as background, give a general overview of the chapter. You may want to use the introduction as a starting point. Be sure to include the following topics:

1. How Do You See the World?
2. Candidates for Renewal
3. Developing Spiritual Vision
4. No More Tears
5. God's Agenda

II. PART TWO
A. BIBLE STUDY APPLICATION

1. Introduction

The Bible Study Application section contains 10 questions that provide an opportunity to examine what the Bible says about the nature and importance of spiritual work.

2. Procedure

Select Small Group Leaders. Ask for volunteers or select three small group leaders. Then assign each small group leader a number from 1-3. (This can be done beforehand to save time.) Ask the small group leaders to write their numbers on large sheets of white paper so that they can be seen from a distance.

Divide into Small Groups. Inform the participants that they will be separated into three small groups. Each group will study a different set of questions and then will present their findings to the larger group at the end of the study period. The questions should be assigned as follows:

> Group #1: Being Renewed (questions 1 through 4)
>
> Group #2: Renewal in Process (questions 5 through 8)
>
> Group #3: Renewal Complete (questions 9 and 10)

Allow Participants to Count Off by Threes. Then ask them to follow the small group leader who is holding their assigned number. Identify the location of each group. (These locations can also be pre-printed on a sheet of paper, photocopied, and distributed to save time.) Participants should then assemble into smaller groups in their respective meeting areas.

B. SMALL GROUP STUDY

1. Small Group Leaders

   Each group will have one topic to explore. For each topic, there are several questions and related Scripture references to stimulate discussion.

2. Sharing Insights

   After 15 minutes, designate someone who will summarize the small group discussion within the larger body of participants. Remind the designated person that she or he will only have two minutes to present.

C. LARGE GROUP PRESENTATIONS

Reconvene the Group. Call the small groups back together.

Explain the Procedure. Explain that a representative of each small group will share that group's reflections on the Bible Study Application questions with the larger group. It may be necessary to pose questions which require them to relate their discussion of Scripture to modern life.

Remind Small Group Representatives of the Time. Remind each group representative that he or she should try to summarize the group's discussion in two minutes. Allow up to two minutes to discuss each group's presentation.

D. LARGE GROUP STUDY*

Personal Application and Church Ministry Discussion. If time permits, the larger group can then discuss the Personal Application and Church Ministry questions together.

1. Introduction

   The Personal Application section contains five question which encourage the participants to consider the teaching in light of their own lives. The Church Ministry section contains three questions which address some implications for the congregation as a whole.

2. Sharing Insights

   This discussion should be open-ended and voluntary. The sharing of personal insights or recommendations for church ministry should be encouraged but not required. The group may have quite a bit to say. Watch the clock! Stop them after 10 minutes.

*Answers are not provided for the Personal Application or Church Ministry sections because of the personal or specific nature of the questions.

E. CLOSING PRAYER
Hold hands, form a circle, and ask for specific prayer requests. Then ask for several volunteers to pray, keeping the prayer requests in mind.

ANSWERS TO BIBLE STUDY APPLICATION

Being Renewed
For a Christian, spiritual renewal is a way of life. It begins when we receive Christ as Lord and Saviour. But we do not become like Him instantly. We are constantly changing and growing to become the people that God wants us to be.

1. Use following verses to describe God's role in the process of spiritual renewal.
    a) God began the work and He will continue to perform it.
    b) God works in us, therefore we can please Him.
    c) God will sanctify and keep us.
    d) God has saved us and called us according to His own purpose and grace.
    e) Jesus is the Author and the Finisher of our faith.
    f) God has given us everything we need for abundant spiritual life.

2. Use the following verses to describe how we are renewed.

    a) Through prayer

    b) By waiting and depending on God

    c) By the work of the Holy Spirit

    d) By the Word of God

3. Use the following verses to describe what part of us we are to renew.

    a) Our hearts and our spirits

    b) Our minds

    c) Our inner selves

4. Use the following verses to describe what part of us we are to offer to God as a spiritual sacrifice.

    a) Our bodies

    b) Our praise

    c) Our good works and generosity

Renewal in Process: Ambassadors for Christ

5. While on earth, we are God's work in process. Use the following verses to identify the purpose of spiritual renewal.

    a) We are being changed into the image of Jesus Christ.

    b) God's nature is being developed in us.

    c) We are to bring others to Christ.

6. Use the following verses to identify the attributes of a renewed heart.

    a) Stable

 b) Knows God

 c) Fruitful

 d) Knows Christ

7. Use the following verses to identify the benefits of a renewed mind.

 a) Life and peace

 b) Having the mind of Christ

8. Use the following verses to identify the requirements for spiritual vision.

 a) We must be pure in heart.

 b) We must be born again.

 c) We must receive revelation from the Holy Spirit.

 d) We must be sanctified by faith in Christ.

 e) We must be saints of God.

Renewal Complete: Citizens of New Jerusalem

9. Use the verses in parentheses to answer the following questions.

 a) Who are we waiting for?

 We are waiting for Jesus Christ.

 b) What are we waiting for?

 We are waiting for the redemption of our bodies.

 c) What will we put on?

 We will put on incorruption and immortality.

 d) Where is our citizenship?

 Our citizenship is in heaven.

 e) What kind of city are we looking for?

 We are looking for a heavenly city whose builder and maker is God.

f) Describe our response.

We will be glad and rejoice.

g) Who will care for us?

The Lord Himself will care for us.

10. Read Revelation 22:3-9. Use these verses to answer the following questions.

a) What shall be removed?

The curse of sin will be removed.

b) What shall be present?

The throne of God and the Lamb will be present.

c) What work will we do?

We will serve God.

d) What will we see?

We will see His face.

e) What will be the only source of light?

God will be our light.

f) Will there be any darkness?

There will be no darkness at all.

g) Who should we worship?

We should worship God alone.

ENDNOTES

Chapter 1

[1] Howard Thurman, *Meditations of the Heart,* San Francisco: Howard Thurman Educational Trust, 1981, pp. 171-172, used by permission.

[2] Henry Mitchell, *Black Beliefs,* New York: Harper and Row Publishers, 1975, p. 139.

[3] Isaac Watts, *New National Baptist Hymnal,* Nashville: National Baptist Publishing Board, 1977, no. 135.

[4] Georgia Harkness, *Religious Living,* New York: Abingdon Press, 1937, pp. 48-51.

[5] Gayraud Wilmore, "Spiritual and Social Transformation as the Vocation of the Black Church," *Churches in Struggle,* New York, William K. Tabb (ed.), Monthly Review Press, 1986, p. 240.

Chapter 2

[6] Howard Thurman, *Meditations of the Heart,* San Francisco: Howard Thurman Educational Trust, 1981, pp. 215-216, used by permission.

Chapter 3

[7] Howard Thurman, *Meditations of the Heart,* San Francisco: Howard Thurman Educational Trust, 1981, used by permission.

Chapter 4

[8] James Melvin Washington, *Conversations With God,* New York: HarperCollins Publishers, Inc., 1994, p. 151.

[9] *Black Writers of America, A Comprehensive Anthology,* New York: Macmillan Publishing Co., 1972, pp. 869-870.

Chapter 5

[10] Howard Thurman, *Meditations of the Heart,* San Francisco: Howard Thurman Educational Trust, 1981, pp. 25-26, used by permission.

[11] Cleveland B. McAffe, *New National Baptist Hymnal,* Nashville: National Baptist Publishing Board, 1977, no. 426.

[12] Hugh Stowell, *Hymnal for Worship and Celebration,* Waco: Word Music Company, 1986, p. 432.

Chapter 6

[13] Howard Thurman, *Meditations of the Heart,* San Francisco: Howard Thurman Educational Trust, 1981, pp. 206-207, used by permission.

[14] Charles Albert Tindley, *New National Baptist Hymnal,* Nashville: National Baptist Publishing Board, 1977, no. 225.

[15] Howard Thurman, *Meditations of the Heart,* San Francisco: Howard Thurman Educational Trust, 1981, p. 206, used by permission.

[16] Myrna Summers, *God Gave Me a Song,* New York: Cotillion Records, Division of Atlantic Recording Company, 1970.

Chapter 7

[17] Howard Thurman, *Meditations of the Heart,* San Francisco: Howard Thurman Educational Trust, 1981, p. 183, used by permission.

Chapter 8

[18] Howard Thurman, *Meditations of the Heart,* San Francisco: Howard Thurman Educational Trust, 1981, pp. 46-47 ,used by permission.

Chapter 9

[19] Howard Thurman, *Meditations of the Heart,* San Francisco: Howard Thurman Educational Trust, 1981, pp. 196-197, used by permission.

Chapter 10

[20] Howard Thurman, *Meditations of the Heart,* San Francisco: Howard Thurman Educational Trust, 1981, p. 163, used by permission.

[21] Dietrich Bonhoeffer, *The Cost of Discipleship,* New York: Macmillan Publishing Company, 1963, p. 45.

Chapter 11

[22] James Melvin Washington, *Conversations With God,* New York: HarperCollins Publishers, Inc., 1994, p. 260.

Chapter 12

[23] James Melvin Washington, *Conversations With God,* New York: HarperCollins Publishers, Inc., 1994, p. 242.

BIBLIOGRAPHY

Bartlett, John. *Familiar Quotes.* Boston: Little, Brown, and Company, 1992.

Black Writers of America, A Comprehensive Anthology, New York: Macmillan Publishing Co., 1972.

Bonhoeffer, Dietrich. *The Cost of Discipleship.* New York: Macmillan Publishing Company, 1963.

Brown, Robert McAfee. *Spirituality and Liberation.* Philadelphia: Westminster Press, 1988.

Bruce, Calvin E. "Black Spirituality and Theological Method." *The Journal of the Interdenominational Theological Center,* vol. 3 (June 1986): 65-76.

_____. "Black Spirituality, Language and Faith." *Journal of Religious Education,* Yale Divinity School, vol. 71 (August 1976): 363-376.

Cone, James H. *Black Theology and Black Power.* New York: Seabury Press, 1969.

_____. *A Black Theology of Liberation* (1st edition). Philadelphia: Lippincott, 1970.

_____. "Black Worship." *The Study of Spirituality.* Cheslyn Jones, Geoffrey Wainwright, and Edward Yarnold (eds.). New York: Oxford University Press, 1986.

_____. *The Spirituals and the Blues: An*

Interpretation. Westport: Greenwood Press, 1980.

Delaney, John J. (trans.). *The Practice of the Presence of God.* (Written by Brother Lawrence of the Resurrection.) Garden City: Image Books, 1977.

Hanson, Bradley (ed.). *Modern Christian Spirituality.* Atlanta: Scholars Press, 1990.

Harkness, Georgia. *Religious Living.* New York: Abingdon Press, 1937.

_____. *The Faith by Which the Church Lives.* New York: Abingdon Press, 1940.

_____. *Mysticism: Its Meaning and Message.* Nashville: Abingdon Press, 1973.

Jones, Major J. *The Color of God: The Concept of God in Afro-American Thought.* Macon: Mercer Press, 1987.

Lovell, John, Jr. *Black Song—The Forge and the Flame: The Story of How the Afro-American Spiritual Was Hammered Out.* New York: Macmillan Publishing Company, 1972.

Mbiti, John S. *African Religions and Philosophy.* Garden City: Doubleday, 1970.

_____. *Concepts of God in Africa.* New York: Praeger Publishers, 1970.

Merton, Thomas. *Contemplative Prayer.* New York: Herder and Herder, 1969.

_____. *Life and Holiness.* Garden City: Image

Books, 1963.

Mitchell, Henry H. *Black Belief: Folk Beliefs of Blacks in America and West Africa* (1st edition). New York: Harper and Row Publishers, 1975.

New National Baptist Hymnal. Nashville: National Baptist Publishing Board, 1977.

Pannenberg, Wolfhart. *Christian Spirituality* (1st edition). Philadelphia: Westminster Press, 1983.

Sobrino, Jon (trans.). *Spirituality of Liberation: Toward Political Holiness.* Maryknoll: Orbis Books, 1988.

Stowell, Hugh. *Hymnal for Worship and Celebration.* Waco: Word Music Company, 1986.

Tabb, William K. (ed.). *Churches in Struggle: Liberation Theologies and Social Change in North America.* New York: Monthly Review Press, 1986.

Thurman, Howard. *Deep is the Hunger: Meditations for Apostles of Sensitiveness.* San Francisco: Howard Thurman Educational Trust.

_____. *Disciplines of the Spirit* (1st edition). San Francisco: Howard Thurman Educational Trust, 1981.

_____. *The Growing Edge.* San Francisco: Howard Thurman Educational Trust, 1981.

_____. *Meditations of the Heart.* San Francisco: Howard Thurman Educational Trust, 1981.

Trulear, Harold D. "The Lord Will Make a Way Somehow: Black Worship and the Afro-American Story." *The Journal of the Interdenominational Theological Center,* vol. 13 (Fall 1985): 87-106.

Underhill, Evelyn. *Mysticism* (12th edition, rev.). London: Methuen, 1930.

_____. *The Mystic Way: A Psychological Study in Christian Origins.* New York: E.P. Dutton, 1913.

_____. *The Spiritual Life.* New York: Harper and Row Publishers, 1936.

_____. *Worship.* New York: Harper and Row Publishers, 1937.

Washington, James Melvin. *Conversations With God.* New York: HarperCollins Publishers, Inc., 1994.

Wilmore, Gayraud S. *Black Religion and Black Radicalism: An Interpretation of the Religious History of Afro-American People.* Maryknoll: Orbis Books, 1983.

_____. "Spirituality and Social Transformation as the Vocation of the Black Church." *Churches in Struggle.* New York: Monthly Review Press, 1986.

Wilmore, Gayraud and James H. Cone (eds.). *Black Theology: A Documentary History 1966-1979.* Maryknoll: Orbis Books, 1979.